ISSUES IN YEAR-ROUND EDUCATION

ISSUES IN YEAR-ROUND EDUCATION

By

MOSSIE J. RICHMOND, Jr.

Dean of the University College, Associate
Professor of Educational Administration,
Arkansas State University

THE CHRISTOPHER PUBLISHING HOUSE
NORTH QUINCY, MASSACHUSETTS

PRINTED IN

THE UNITED STATES OF AMERICA

To

Velmar, Deryle, and Reché who make it all worthwhile

and

In memory of my father, Mossie J. Richmond, Sr.

PREFACE

If we were to compile a list of long-standing educational issues, I am certain that year-round education would rank near or at the top of that list. This issue has been with us for more than three-quarters of a century, and we seem to be no closer to a resolution of the key questions surrounding the concept than we were in the first decade of this century. My attempt to resolve the wide range of issues related to year-round education—a task that no other individual had been successful in accomplishing—evolved as a series of accidental educational blunders rather than through conscious intent. Although the topic of year-round education or the extended school year was of great interest to me, my initial plan was to focus my research upon the first ten issues listed below. The purposes to which I had delimited my investigation were: (1) to identify schools and/or school corporations in which extended school year or year-round school programs were currently in operation in each of the fifty states of the United States of America; (2) to identify schools and/or school districts in which extended school year or year-round school programs had been implemented and abandoned since 1956; (3) to identify schools and/or school districts in which extended school year or year-round school programs were to be implemented in the near future; (4) to determine the type of extended school year or year-round school designs conducted or to be conducted in each school corporation identified as part of the study population; (5) to determine the rationale for implementation of the extended school year concept in each school corporation; (6) to determine the extent to which each type of extended school year or year-round school plan had made each rationale for implementation of the program a reality within the districts in which the extended school year or year-round school plans were currently in operation, were to be implemented in the near future, or had been abandoned since 1956; (7) to determine the administrative problems faced by administrators of extended school year programs; (8) to determine the sources of additional revenue for the implementation and maintenance of extended school year programs; (9) to determine teacher preference for employment in extended school year programs; and (10) to determine community acceptance of extended school year programs.

As I embarked upon the task of reading through the literature related to the year-round school concept, I found myself being launched into an educational stupor by investing hundreds of hours over a twelve-month period trying to wade through the mountains of materials written on year-round education since the turn of the century. When I awakened from my educational slumber to construct my survey instruments, I subconsciously had expanded my study to include an additional seventeen elusive, insurmountable, and difficult questions that had to be addressed and answered with many qualifications based upon the extended school year design, variations of the designs, and the number of variables applied to the designs in each year-round school program. These issues are as follows: (1) Does the extended school year or year-round school concept actually save money? (2) Which extended school year or year-round plan is likely to save the greatest amount of money? (3) Are curriculum improvements possible in extended school year or year-round school situations? (4) Which extended school year or year-round school plan permits the greatest curriculum improvements? (5) Which extended school year or year-round school plan is most acceptable to the tax-paying public as perceived by central office personnel? (6) Does the extended school year or year-round school concept decrease the student attrition rate and increase the retention rate? (7) Which extended school year or year-round school plan has the most positive effect upon decreasing the student attrition rate and increasing the retention rate? (8) Does the extended school year or year-round concept permit acceleration of bright students and present opportunities for reluctant learners to maintain or acquire desirable grade level or learning expectations? (9) Which extended school year or year-round school plan permits the greatest opportunities for bright students and reluctant learners? (10) Which extended school year or year-round school plan causes the greatest number of administrative problems? (11) Which extended school year or year-round school plan causes the greatest number of problems in scheduling students into extracurricular school activities? (12) Which plan is most attractive to teachers, especially male teachers and heads of households? (13) Which extended school year or year-round plan provides maximum utilization of educational facilities and resources? (14) Does year-round education deter juvenile delinquency, and, if so, which plan has the greatest impact on reducing juvenile delinquency? (15) Which extended

school year or year-round school plan provides the greatest continuity of learning by pupils? (16) What are the effects of year-
round or extended school year attendance upon the mental,
physical, and social well-being of teachers and students?

As a result of including items in the survey instrument that
sought answers to the previous questions, we now have within
the pages of this book a comprehensive discussion of the current
and historical issues surrounding the year-round school movement,
the responses of school administrators to the issues listed on the
survey instrument, and my analysis of the data reported by the
school administrators who were currently conducting extended
school year or year-round programs.

TABLE OF CONTENTS

9

LIST OF TABLES

11

ISSUES IN YEAR-ROUND EDUCATION

Essay One

CURRENT STATUS OF THE EXTENDED SCHOOL YEAR

Based upon responses from 131 (89 percent) of the 147 school administrators contacted in a nationwide survey of extended school year programs, there were more extended school year programs currently in operation in the United States of America than at any previous period of time in the history of the nation. School officials in forty-eight school districts, in one university laboratory school, and in one private school in twenty-one states were currently conducting extended school year programs at the time of the investigation (see Table I), and school officials in twenty-eight school districts and in one university laboratory school in eleven states were scheduled to implement extended school year programs as of September, 1973 (see Table II). Extended school year programs had been implemented and later abandoned in approximately six school districts in five states since 1968 (see Table III).

By early 1974, extended school year programs were in operation in at least one school building in approximately seventy-six school districts, in two university laboratory schools, and in one private school in twenty-five states throughout the U.S. Currently there are twelve basic extended school year designs in operation in the United States of America: (1) the Forty-Five—Fifteen or the Nine-Three; (2) the Continuous Four-Quarter; (3) the Quinmester or the Pentamester; (4) the Continuous School Year design; (5) the Flexible All-Year; (6) the Quadrimester; (7) the Rotating Trimester; (8) Concept Six; (9) the Extended K-Twelve; (10) the Four-One-Four-One-One; (11) the Sixty-Twenty; and (12) the Rotating Four-Quarter. The first articulation of a four-term school year or a year-round or extended school year design in continuous operation was set forth in an article by Irwin Shepard in 1898. Shepard was, at that time, president of Winona Normal School (Winona State College), Winona, Minnesota; he was also the first full-time executive secretary of the NEA. Authorities generally agree that the first

TABLE I

CURRENTLY OPERATING EXTENDED SCHOOL YEAR DESIGNS

State	45-15	9-3	Flexible All-Year	Continuous School Year	Quadrimester	Quinmester	Continuous Four Quarter	Trimester	Extended K-12	Other Variations	Total	Percentage of Total
Arizona	0	0	0	0	0	0	1	0	0	0	1	2
California	14	0	1	0	1	0	1	0	0	0	17	34
Colorado	1	0	0	0	0	0	0	0	0	0	1	2
Florida	1	0	0	1	0	1	1	0	2	0	6	12
Georgia	0	0	0	0	0	0	1	0	0	0	1	2
Illinois	2	0	0	0	0	0	0	0	0	0	2	4
Kansas	0	0	0	0	0	0	0	0	0	1	1	2
Kentucky	0	0	0	0	0	0	1	0	0	0	1	2
Michigan	1	0	0	0	0	1	0	0	0	0	2	4
Missouri	0	1	0	0	0	0	0	0	0	0	1	2
Minnesota	1	0	0	0	0	1	0	0	0	0	2	4
New Hampshire	0	0	0	0	0	0	1	0	0	0	1	2
New York	0	0	0	1	0	0	0	0	0	0	1	2
North Carolina	1	0	0	0	0	0	1	0	0	0	2	4
Oregon	1	0	0	0	0	0	0	0	0	0	1	2
Pennsylvania	0	0	0	0	0	0	1	0	0	0	1	2
Texas	0	0	0	0	0	0	1	1	0	0	2	4
Utah	0	0	0	1	0	0	1	0	0	1	3	6
Vermont	1	0	0	0	0	0	0	0	0	0	1	2
Virginia	1	0	0	0	0	0	0	0	0	0	1	2
Washington	0	0	0	0	0	0	0	0	0	1	1	2
West Virginia	0	0	0	0	0	0	0	0	0	1	1	2
TOTAL	24	1	1	3	1	3	10	1	2	4	50	100

implementation of the Shepard concept of an extended school year design (the rotating four-quarter plan) occurred in an elementary school in Bluffton, Indiana, in 1904. Since that time approximately 191 extended school year programs have been implemented in this country. Seventy-nine programs, or 41 percent of all those ever implemented in this country, are currently in operation. Twenty-four programs, or 30 percent of the seventy-nine currently in operation, exist in the schools of California. California is followed by Florida and Arizona, with six programs or 8 percent of the current

TABLE II

EXTENDED SCHOOL YEAR DESIGNS TO BE IMPLEMENTED
IN THE 1973-74 SCHOOL YEAR

State	45-15	Flexible All-Year	Continuous School Year	Quadrimester	Quinmester	Continuous Four Quarter	Trimester	Concept Six	60-20	Rotating Four Quarter	Other Variations	Total	Percentage of Total
Arizona	5	0	0	0	0	0	0	0	0	1	0	6	20.69
California	4	0	0	0	0	0	1	0	1	0	1	7	24.14
Colorado	0	0	0	0	0	0	0	2	0	0	0	2	06.90
Michigan	0	0	0	1	0	0	0	0	0	0	0	1	03.45
Montana	0	0	0	0	1	0	0	0	0	0	0	1	03.45
New Hampshire	0	0	0	0	0	1	0	0	0	0	0	1	03.45
Ohio	1	0	0	0	0	0	0	0	0	0	0	1	03.45
Oregon	1	0	0	0	0	0	0	0	0	0	0	1	03.45
Pennsylvania	0	1	0	0	0	1	0	0	0	0	0	2	06.90
South Carolina	0	0	0	0	3	0	0	0	0	0	0	3	10.34
Virginia	1	1	1	0	1	0	0	0	0	0	0	4	13.79
TOTAL	12	2	1	1	5	2	1	2	1	1	1	29	100.01

TABLE III

EXTENDED SCHOOL YEAR DESIGNS IMPLEMENTED
AND ABANDONED SINCE 1968

State	45-15	Continuous Four Quarter	Extended K-12	Other Varia- tions	Total	Percent- age of Total
California	0	0	0	1	1	16.67
Florida	0	0	1	0	1	16.67
Oregon	1	1	0	0	2	33.33
South Dakota	1	0	0	0	1	16.67
West Virginia	0	0	0	1	1	16.67
TOTAL	2	1	1	2	6	100.01

operations each. At least one extended school year program is to be found in twenty-five of the fifty states.

Officials of the NEA have reported that at least sixty different extended school year designs and variations of designs have been developed during the past three-quarters of a century.

Although the total number of school administrators who have quietly and cautiously conducted investigations into the feasibility of extending the school year is unknown, feasibility studies were reported to have been conducted in at least ninety-nine school districts since 1968, excluding the eighty-two school districts, two university laboratory schools, and one private school mentioned in this article.

School administrators reported that 687 elementary schools, 64 middle schools, 105 junior high schools, 18 junior-senior high schools, 114 high schools, 3 K-twelve schools, 1 vocational-technical school, and 1 school for the trainable retarded were being conducted on an extended school year schedule.

School officials in only five of the school districts had scheduled all schools of the district on an extended school year calendar. School officials had implemented and abandoned extended school year programs in at least seven elementary schools, one middle school, one junior high school, and one vocational-technical school since 1968. The greatest concentration of effort in the extended school year movement seems to be focused upon the elementary grades.

The total student population in sixty-four of the seventy-nine school corporations in which extended school year programs were in operation was 1,693,441 according to responses from school administrators. Approximately 28 percent of the total student population in sixty-four of the school corporations (468,087 students) was enrolled in extended school year programs.

Proponents of the extended school year concept have argued that male teachers and heads of households prefer employment in extended school year programs because of increased earning possibilities. Administrators in school corporations, where extended school year programs provided opportunities for increased earning, agreed with the assertion of the proponents. If the following data on teacher employment patterns and preferences are representative of the entire extended school year study population, male teachers and heads of households comprise a small percentage of the entire teaching staff employed in extended school year programs. The total number of teachers employed in sixty-one of the school corporations (72 percent of the school corporations in

the study population) was 69,218. In forty-seven school corporations (55 percent of the corporations studied), school officials had
employed 2,841 teachers for an extended number of days during
the calendar year. The number of male teachers employed in thirty-
one school corporations (36 percent of the study population) was
8,532. The number of male teachers employed on extended school
year contracts in the thirty-one school corporations was 509 (6
percent of the total number of male teachers employed in the corporations). Twenty-five school administrators (29 percent of the
study population) reported that 6,422 of the teachers in the school
corporations were heads of households and that 572 (9 percent
of the heads of households) were employed on extended school
year contracts. The number of heads of households from the study
population who were also men is not currently known. The reported
preferences of male teachers and heads of households for employment on extended school year or year-round contracts are shown
in Table IV.

TABLE IV

TEACHER PREFERENCE REGARDING
YEAR-ROUND EMPLOYMENT

Responses	Men	Percentage of Total	Heads of Households	Percentage of Total
Prefer Extended Contract	32	40.51	32	40.51
No Response	30	37.97	18	22.78
Do Not Desire ESY Contract	9	11.39	11	13.92
Contract Preference Unknown	4	5.06	9	11.39
Too Soon to Determine	2	2.53	2	2.53
ESY Employment Not a Feature of the Design	2	2.53	2	2.53
Data Not Available	0	0.00	3	3.80
No Increase in the Number of Teaching Days in the District	0	0.00	2	2.53
Total	79	99.99	79	99.99

The reasons cited for implementation of the extended school year
programs in the various school corporations are listed in sequence

according to the frequency of responses from the seventy-nine administrators who had been involved in extended school year programs since 1968: (1) to make better utilization of costly plant facilities which were largely unused or underused during the three months of summer; (2) to improve and reorganize the curriculum; (3) to provide enrichment courses to the curriculum; (4) to prevent the loss of learning by students during the summer vacation; (5) to save money by reducing the amount of school plant space and the number of facilities needed to house students; (6) to make better utilization of the time of pupils during the summer, thereby reducing juvenile delinquency; (7) to conduct experiments on the effects of year-round programs on the emotional and physical well-being of students and teachers; (8) to save money by delaying school construction costs and, thus, eliminating the need to ask taxpayers to support new bond issues; (9) to reduce the student attrition rate; (10) to provide a solution to crowded conditions while needed buildings were being completed; (11) to help the disadvantaged students maintain or acquire acceptable grade level or learning expectations; (12) to give teachers employment during the summer months, thus, increasing teacher salaries and professional status; (13) to save money by reducing the number of pupils required to repeat a grade, thereby reducing the school enrollment; (14) to save money by permitting the acceleration of bright pupils resulting in a saving of one, two, or three years of schooling in twelve; (15) to make teaching in the district more attractive to male teachers through greater earning possibilities; (16) to force the community to provide needed funds for school construction; (17) to improve educational achievement; (18) to meet increasing enrollment; (19) to acquire needed space; (20) to eliminate double sessions; and (21) to give students more options (see Appendix B).

The most significant reasons for implementation of extended school year programs were identified and are presented in decreasing order of significance: (1) to improve and reorganize the curriculum; (2) to make better utilization of costly plant facilities largely unused or underused during the three months of summer; (3) to add enrichment courses to the curriculum; (4) to provide a solution to crowded conditions while needed buildings were being completed; (5) to prevent loss of learning during the summer vacation; (6) to save money by reducing the number of school plants and facilities needed; (7) to save money by delaying construction costs and, thus, eliminating the need to ask taxpayers to support bond issues; (8) to help the disadvantaged catch up; (9) to save money by reducing the number of pupils who were required to repeat a grade, reducing enrollment; (10) to make better utilization of the time of pupils during the summer months, reducing juvenile delinquency; (11) to conduct experiments on the effects of year-round or extended school year programs; (12) to give teachers employment during the summer months, thus increasing teacher salaries and professional status; (13) to save money by permitting the acceleration of bright pupils resulting in savings of years of schooling per accelerated pupil; (14) to make teaching in the district more attractive to men through greater earning possibilities; (15) to reduce the dropout rate; (16) to meet increasing enrollment; (17) to improve academic achievement; (18) to improve educational opportunities; (19) to acquire needed space; (20) to force the community to provide needed funds for school construction; and (21) to give students more options (see Appendix C).

Additional funding for the implementation and maintenance of extended school year programs has come from a variety of sources and combinations of sources. More than $1,031,026.16 of the additional funds over the past five years had come from ESEA Title III sources in fourteen states, and $950,000 in additional funds had been made available from state sources in two states. The data presented in Table V indicate the current sources of additional funding for extended school year programs in sixty-nine of the eighty-five school corporations.

Some writers have reported that extending the school year could provide local school officials a means of securing additional funds to solve a local school corporation's finance related problems and could eliminate the need for the immediate acquisition of additional local school support for the program or for continued operation on a traditional school year calendar. Twenty-six school administrators (33 percent) of the seventy-nine administrators comprising the study population had found the previous assertion to be true. However, twenty-two administrators (28 percent) were able to eliminate neither the need for additional local funds through implementation of the extended school year programs nor through the acquisition of additional sources of funds. Twenty-seven administrators (34 percent) did not respond to the question on the extent to which the acquisition of additional sources of funds eliminated the need for additional local school support, and two school administrators reported that the question was not applicable to the local school situation.

Thirty-six school administrators (46 percent) reported that extended school year programs would have been implemented in their school corporations had outside sources of additional revenue not been available. Seventeen administrators (22 percent) felt that extended school year programs would not have been

TABLE V

SOURCES OF FUNDING EXTENDED
SCHOOL YEAR PROGRAMS

Source of Fundings	Number of Districts	Percentage of Total Population
Local tax levies and regular state allocation	34	43
No response	14	18
Federal funds (ESEA)	11	14
Federal funds, local tax levies, and regular state allocation	5	6
Student tuition	2	3
Local tax levies and student tuition	2	3
Federal funds, local tax levies, student tuition, and regular state allocation	2	3
Regular state allocation and special state grants	2	3
Special federal grants	1	1
Regular state allocation	1	1
Federal funds, student tuition, regular state allocations, and seed money from the state	1	1
Federal funds, local tax levies, student tuition, regular state allocation, and special state grants	1	1
Federal funds, local tax levies, regular state allocation, and special state grants	1	1
Special state grants	1	1
Federal funds and regular state allocation	1	1
TOTAL	79	100

implemented in their districts without outside sources of additional revenue; and twenty administrators (25 percent) did not report on the extent to which outside sources of additional revenue figured into the decisions of school corporation officials to implement the extended school year program.

Some writers have reported that many school officials were forced to implement extended school year programs when the school districts were at the legal maximum bonded indebtedness and additional revenue for needed capital outlay could not be raised for continued operation of schools on a traditional school year schedule or when the school community had defeated a bond issue designed to acquire needed revenue for capital outlay. In eleven school corporations (14 percent of the study population), community people had rejected a bond issue which necessitated the implementation of an extended school year program. In forty-two school corporations (53 percent of the study population), community people had not rejected a bond issue when extended school year programs were implemented. School administrators in twenty-four school corporations (30 percent of the study population) did not report data on the passage or failure of bond issues in the community. Fourteen school corporations (18 percent) were at the legal maximum bonded indebtedness when extended school year programs were implemented, and forty-three (54 percent) of the corporations were not at the legal maximum bonded indebtedness. Twenty administrators (25 percent) did not respond to the question on the legal limits of the district's bonding authority.

Extended school year programs generally have not resulted in financial savings in the school budget. If the extended school year program provided schooling for an additional number of days during the calendar year, the total expenditures for the schools scheduled on an extended school year basis increased when compared to the same schools scheduled on a conventional school year calendar. The extent of the increase in the cost of conducting an extended school year program is influenced by the type of extended school year design selected for implementation and the number of cost saving variables applied to the operation by school officials. Financial savings through implementation of an extended school year program should be measured in terms of projected expenditures for continued operation on a conventional school year calendar. These projected expenditures seem to result in short-term savings and justify extending the school year only when the cost of constructing and operating new school buildings, staffing new school buildings, and the purchase of additional facilities and supplies are required for continued operation on a conventional school year schedule. Unless implementation of an extended school year program eliminates the need for spending large sums of money in capital outlay in the foreseeable future, an anticipated financial savings is not likely to be a justifiable reason for extending the school year over an extended period of time. However, a rapid increase in the number of students to be housed by a school corporation may cause school officials to view certain school year designs as a feasible solution to the housing problem.

Historically, state legislation and school codes have been re-

TABLE VI

REPORTED STATE FINANCIAL AND LEGISLATIVE CONSIDERATIONS
ON THE EXTENDED SCHOOL YEAR

States	Special Grant From State to Finance Extended School Year Operations	State Laws Restrict Flexibility in Extending the Length of the School Year	Extended School Year Permissive Legislation Enacted	State School Officials Applied for Federal Funds to Offset Additional Cost of Extended School Year Operations	State Officials Received Federal Funds to Offset Additional Cost of Extended School Year Operations	Local District Officials Received Federal Funds to Offset Additional Cost of Extended School Year Operations
Alabama		No	No	No	No	
Alaska		No	No	No	No	
California		Yes	Yes	Yes	Yes	Yes
Colorado		Yes	No	No	Yes	Yes
Connecticut		No	Yes	No	No	
Delaware		No	Yes	No	Yes	
Georgia		Yes	No	No	No	
Idaho		No	No	No	No	
Illinois		No	Yes	Yes	Yes	
Indiana	Yes	Yes	Yes	No	No	
Iowa		No	No	No	No	
Kansas		No	No	No	No	
Kentucky		Yes	Yes	No	No	Yes
Maine		No	Yes	No	Yes	Yes
Maryland		No	No	No	No	
Michigan		Yes	No	Yes	Yes	
Minnesota		No	No	No	No	
Missouri		Yes	No	No	No	
Montana		No	No	No	No	
Nebraska		Yes	In Process	No	No	
New Hampshire		No	No	No	No	Yes
New Jersey		No	No	No	Yes	
New Mexico		No	Yes	No	No	
North Carolina		Yes	No	No	Yes	
Ohio		Yes	Yes	Yes	Yes	
Oklahoma		Yes	No	No	No	
Oregon		No	Yes	No	No	
Pennsylvania	Yes	Yes	No	No	Yes	
Rhode Island		No	No	No	Yes	Yes
South Carolina		Yes	Yes	Yes	Yes	
South Dakota		No	No	No	No	
Tennessee		Yes	Yes	No	No	

Utah	No	Yes	No	Yes	Yes
Vermont	No	No	No	No	
Virginia	No	No	No	No	
Washington	Yes	No	No	No	Yes
West Virginia	No	Yes	No	No	
Wisconsin	No	Yes	No	No	
Wyoming	Yes	No	No	No	
No Response	Eleven State School Officials				

strictive to the implementation, maintenance, and financing of various extended school year designs. The data in Table VI summarize the current activity and flexibility permitted in thirty-nine (78 percent) of the states concerning extended school year operations.

Although community opposition to the extended school year concept is considered a real problem in implementing the program by many administrators, it is interesting to note that community opposition decreases in proportion to the length of time the program continues in operation. Only one school administrator of the seventy-nine administrators included in this survey had encountered an increase in community opposition to the extended school year program since the program was implemented. Selection or development of the most appropriate extended school year design for implementation in a given community may be a factor in community acceptance of the program. Different extended school year designs have been developed and must be selected or modified to accomplish different objectives in varying degrees. Selection of an inappropriate extended school year design may prove impractical and fail to accomplish the objectives or solve the problems in a given community. Community opposition to an ill-selected or ill-designed plan may be an expected result.

The study population for this investigation was identified by forty-eight (96 percent) of the fifty state school superintendents in the United States, officials of the National Education Association, and, through a review of the literature, related to the extended school year concept.

OPERATIONAL DESIGNS FOR EXTENDING
THE LENGTH OF THE TRADITIONAL
SCHOOL YEAR

Many extended school year designs and variations of designs have been developed, modified, and implemented since the concept of a closely articulated four-term school year in continuous operation was first set forth in an article by Irwin Shepard, President of Winona Normal School (Winona State College), Winona, Minnesota, in 1898. Authorities generally agree that the first implementation of an extended school year design in an elementary school occurred in Bluffton, Indiana, in 1904. Since the implementation of the Rotating Four-Quarter plan in Bluffton, many other rotating-term or cycle extended school year designs have been developed, selected, and modified to accomplish specific objectives or to resolve a series of school related problems in respective school communities.

The type of year-round or extended school year program adopted in one community will not necessarily solve the problems or work in another community. Year-round services must be suited to the needs and purposes of the particular community in which the plans are to be implemented. In a school district in which officials are contemplating school year reorganization, the officials should consider all alternatives and select the year-round plan which seems to best meet the perceived needs of the district with the greatest balance of advantages over disadvantages. The need of the school district should be analyzed before a particular plan is selected.[1] Because of the validity of the previous assertion, many extended school year designs and variations of designs have been developed over the years. A number of approaches to a year-round educational program have claimed considerable attention. Some of the designs and variations of designs have been tried in the field. Unless the extended school year designs are defined, the merits or weaknesses of any one design are likely to be confused with the strengths and liabilities of other designs.

The discussions which follow have appeared in the literature to describe some of the basic designs and some of the many variations currently in operation in the United States.

Extended school year designs and variations of designs currently in operation in the United States of America which constitute the rotating-term or cycle category are: (1) the Forty-Five—Fifteen; (2) the Nine-Three; (3) the Sixty-Twenty; (4) the Rotating Four-Quarter; and (5) the Rotating Trimester.

Other more recently developed extended school year designs have permitted more options and flexibility for the students, parents, and teachers of a community than the rotating-term or cycle designs have traditionally permitted. Extended school year designs currently in operation in the United States which comprise the more flexible category are: (1) the Flexible All-Year; (2) the Quinmester; (3) the Continuous Four-Quarter; (4) the Pentamester; (5) Concept Six; and (6) the Four-One-Four-One-One.

Other extended school year plans currently in operation which do not conform to either of the previous categories are: (1) the Quadrimester; (2) the Extended K-Twelve; and (3) the Continuous School Year designs. A choice of attendance and vacation terms is not a component of these designs; however, opportunities for student acceleration, remediation, and enrichment as well as increased educational opportunities are presented. Opportunities for teacher employment beyond the traditional number of school days during a calendar year are also characteristic of these designs.

The flexibility for students generally presented in the more flexible extended school year designs includes a choice of attendance and vacation periods; a choice of school attendance for a period of time to exceed the traditional number of school days; opportunities for acceleration, remediation, and enrichment; or increased educational opportunities. Advantages for teachers generally found in the more flexible designs are a choice of vacation and employment periods and opportunities for extended school year employment. However, year-round employment or optional vacation periods can be permitted for all or for a percentage of the teachers in a school district through implementation of a rotating-term or cycle design. The employment and vacation regulations would depend upon the student enrollment each school term, the extended school year design implemented, opportunities for extended school year attendance, and the needs and desires of the local school community.

On a nonrotating basis, any of the rotating-term or cycle plans could accommodate mandatory attendance for all students throughout the calendar year if needed classroom space for students is not a problem. Mandatory attendance for a number of terms equal to the traditionally required number of school days with optional attendance for the additional term or terms could also be achieved. A student could be permitted to select his own attendance terms as long as his selection of attendance terms comprised the minimum number of days for school attendance required by state law and local school board regulations.

Rotating-Term or Cycle Designs

There are many variations of rotating-term or cycle designs. Most variations originated during the past few years. Rotating-term or cycle plans were the most publicized of all extended school designs. The primary goal of these variations is the release of classroom space to accommodate more students on a year-round basis. The rotating-term or cycle plan usually contains no provisions for acceleration. Some widely publicized examples of cycling designs are the Forty-Five—Fifteen plan of the Valley View District in Lockport, Illinois; the Nine-Three plan used in the Becky David School in St. Charles County, Missouri; the Forty-Five —Fifteen plan of the Chula Vista District in California; the Twelve-Four plan proposed for Montgomery County, Maryland; and the Eight-Two plan advocated by the New York Department of Education. All of the previous plans have a similar structure, and the difference between the plans is the number of days a student attends class prior to taking a vacation period.[2]

The vast majority of the rotating-term or cycle extended school year designs were developed and implemented as a solution to the housing problems faced by school officials in districts with rapid increases in the number of students to be housed in school facilities. These rotating-term or cycle designs permit a percentage of the student population in a community to attend school and a percentage to take vacations from school on a rotating basis throughout the calendar year. The attendance and vacation patterns for students are usually influenced by the extended school year design and the attendance and vacation regulations adopted by school officials in a given community. Extended school year designs and variations of designs in the United States of America which constitute the rotating-term or cycle category are discussed in subsequent pages.

The Four-Quarter Plan

The four-quarter concept divided the calendar year into four quarters for school operations. In one version, students were divided into four groups; each group attended school for three consecutive quarters and vacationed for the next quarter. Teachers were hired for three quarters and had the option of teaching a fourth quarter for extra pay. In a second version of the four-quarter plan, students were required to attend all four quarters (Compulsory Four-Quarter plan), less a month for vacation, or were required to attend three quarters with the fourth quarter attendance optional. Teachers had the same attendance requirements and options as students.[3]

The four-quarter plan was first put into operation in Bluffton, Indiana, in 1904 and was discontinued in 1915. During the 1920's more than a dozen school systems were conducted year-round, but by 1930 the number of school officials conducting the four-quarter plan had dwindled to six; and by 1950, only Chattanooga, Tennessee, was on the four-quarter plan. Since World War II, many community officials have entertained the possibility of adopting the four-quarter plan with pupils attending three of the four rotating quarters. A few of the studies conducted since World War II have indicated that the plan would probably accomplish the primary purpose—economy.

Although the four-quarter plan has been instituted in some communities from time to time and many studies of the feasibility of implementing the four-quarter plan have been conducted, the design was not known to be in operation in the United States in 1962.[4] Since that time, however, the four-quarter plan has been implemented in some school districts.

According to writers for the School of Education at the University of Florida, the four-quarter plan was one of the better known designs for providing additional use of school buildings. The school calendar is divided into four terms (quarters) of approximately twelve weeks each. The students are divided into four groups, with three groups in attendance and one group on vacation each quarter. The attendance period for each student is approximately 180 days. Officials in numerous school systems have used the four-quarter plan during the past fifty years. The four-quarter plan has not been popular with most students and parents because vacation periods are arbitrarily assigned, and only one group of students can have vacation during the traditional summer vacation period. Although officials in many schools have implemented and abandoned the four-quarter plan, very few school officials currently consider the plan feasible.[5]

The Staggered or Rotating Four-Quarter Plan

For many years, the most prominent all-year school plan was the rotating or staggered four-quarter plan. The rotating four-quarter plan divides the school year into four equal quarters of approximately sixty days or twelve weeks each. Each pupil attends three consecutive quarters and vacations the fourth. Each pupil spends the same amount of time attending school as a student usually would have spent in the traditional nine-month school year arrangements, but the school is in operation throughout the entire year. The vacation periods for students are staggered throughout the calendar year in a manner which results in having three-fourths of the entire student enrollment in attendance and the remaining one-fourth on vacation during any quarter of the year.[6]

Teachers are employed for three quarters or for all four quarters, depending upon the employment arrangements made between the board of education and the individual teacher. Teachers are occasionally employed for fewer than three quarters, although advocates of the plan recommend employment on a four-quarter basis. With four-quarter teacher employment arrangements, there are about forty-eight work weeks in the year, with approximately thirty days left for vacation.[7]

According to White, the obvious advantage of the staggered or rotating four-quarter plan is the ability to accommodate 25 percent more pupils with the same staff, classrooms, laboratories, libraries, and playgrounds. The need for new buildings and equipment under the rotating four-quarter plan is reduced, and better annual salaries are paid to teachers who are employed for all four quarters.

For efficiency, the rotating four-quarter plan requires the total enrollment of school pupils to be about equal for each quarter. The number of students enrolled in each grade in the elementary school and in each subject in the high school should be approximately the same during each quarter. Thus, the rotating four-quarter plan is not designed for efficient implementation by officials in school districts which do not have a large enrollment.

Painting and repair of buildings in a rotating quarter situation must be carried out on weekends and at night at greatly increased costs. Difficulties are also encountered in scheduling interscholastic sports. The rotating four-quarter plan of operation has been abandoned in school districts because of some of the difficulties mentioned. The reasons given do not suggest that the rotating four-quarter plan should not be considered strongly in the future by the large school systems of the nation.[8]

Forty-Five—Fifteen Plan (45-15 or 9-3)

The Forty-Five—Fifteen plan has appeared to be gaining acceptance across the country, especially among officials in the small, rapidly growing suburban school districts. Basically, implementation of the Forty-Five—Fifteen concept places schools into operation year-round but does not increase the actual number of days of attendance for students nor permit students to accelerate their progress through school. The Forty-Five—Fifteen plan simply provides greater classroom utilization and increases the effective use of space by approximately one-third.[9]

The term Forty-Five—Fifteen was derived from the fact that each student in such a system attends school for forty-five days (nine weeks) and is on vacation for fifteen school days (three weeks). At any given moment, one quarter of the students in a school on the Forty-Five—Fifteen are on vacation. There are some common vacation periods for all students, such as Christmas, during which the entire school is shut down. Teachers have a number of employment options: take the same vacation periods as students, work a longer school year at a per diem increase in pay, work a shorter year or shorter days, or teach "intersession" courses during the three-week vacation periods. The most common pattern is for teachers to work the same forty-five—fifteen (nine-three) schedule that students attend.[10]

The Forty-Five—Fifteen or Nine-Three plan is a modification of the staggered or rotating four-quarter plan. The student population is divided into four equal groups, and no two groups vacation at the same time. By staggering the entrance date for each of the four groups of students by fifteen days, the first group which entered school will complete forty-five days of instruction and will begin a fifteen-day or three-week vacation on the day the fourth group enrolls. Fifteen days or three weeks later, when the first group to enter school returns from vacation, the second group to enter school will go on vacation. The cycle is continued until all four groups have entered school and have taken a vacation. Only three-fourths of the student body is in school at any given time.[11]

The Forty-Five—Fifteen is an expression of the number of days of instruction per pupil and the number of days of vacation per pupil. The Nine-Three concept expresses the same period of time in weeks of instruction per pupil and weeks of vacation per pupil.[12] (See Essay Seven.)

The Trimester Plan

In the Trimester plan the school year is divided into three trimesters of sixty-eight to seventy-five days. Each trimester provides the same amount of instructional time as regular semesters through an adjustment in the length of class periods. In many schools, the adjustment is accomplished by reducing the number of class periods rather than extending the school day.

The Trimester designs were favored by persons interested in year-round school programs because new flow patterns, based upon a reduction in enrollments, are established quickly; classroom space becomes available in one and one-third years; teacher time is released in one and one-third years; the Trimester plan becomes self-sustaining in the second year; and from one to three extra terms are included in the designs over a period of years.[13] Three seventy- to seventy-five day trimesters form the foundation of the Trimester plan, as employed at the Florida State University Laboratory School.[14]

The Florida State Trimester plan was designed primarily for acceleration of student programs. A lengthened school year of 210 days was divided into three segments (trimesters) of equal length. Students were required to attend all three terms. One and one-half traditional academic school years of work could be completed in one year. Proponents of the plan did not advocate such rapid acceleration. Instead, proponents recommended using many of the extra terms for enrichment, remediation, work experiences, or to lighten student loads during the regular sessions. Although many college officials experimented with the design, the literature contained only one example of public schools using the trimester approach to scheduling the school year. The one example was Nova High School, Fort Lauderdale, Florida, which was opened in 1963 using a 220-day Trimester. The Nova Trimester plan, however, was dropped by school officials after the first year of operation. In 1966, the 210-day Trimester was tried in Nova High School. Nova officials have now abandoned the Trimester in favor of a 200-day Continuous School Year.[15]

The Rotating Trimester

The Rotating Trimester plan is very similar to the rotating quarter plan. The plan was designed to use school facilities year-round and to increase the capacity of the school buildings. The school calendar is divided into three terms of approximately sixteen weeks each. Students are divided into three groups, with two groups in attendance and one group on vacation each trimester. Using a time equalization factor and a lengthened school day, the work of a normal school year can be completed in two trimesters. As is the case with the rotating quarter plan, the students usually have no attendance options. Students are required to attend two terms and then to vacation for one term. Due to the long period of time pupils are placed on vacation, the public is not likely to accept such a plan.[16]

The Twelve-Four Trimester

A Twelve-Four Trimester provides each student with approximately 180 days of school in a calendar year on a rotating or staggered basis. Each student or group of students receives four weeks of vacation at the end of each twelve-week trimester of instruction. The students are divided into four groups for staggered enrollment and vacation purposes.

Another variation of the Twelve-Four plan also divides the school population, but preserves the unity of each academic trimester with a different distribution of staff holidays. The Twelve-Four variation plan provides, with variations, 180, 185, or 190 school days per group of students. Students are divided into four groups and are enrolled at four-week intervals during the first trimester. The same one-month vacation per group is provided on a rotating or staggered basis following the completion of course work for a trimester.[17]

The Sixty-Twenty Plan

The Sixty-Twenty rotating cycle plan was to be implemented in one district in California in the 1973-74 school year. Prior to consideration of the Sixty-Twenty plan, school officials in the district had not implemented any other type of extended school year plan. The Sixty-Twenty is designed for sixty days or twelve weeks of school attendance and twenty days or four weeks of vacation from school on a rotating basis.

The Quinmester or Pentamester Plan

In a Quinmester or Pentamester plan, 20 percent of the student population may be on vacation and 80 percent is in school at all times.[18] The Quinmester is a plan designed, primarily, not for acceleration, but for increased plant utilization. The lengthened school year is divided into five forty-five-day sessions. Pupil attendance may be required for four of the five sessions, with

optional attendance during the fifth session. Students who attend
all sessions can accelerate through academic programs. School
officials of Dade County, Florida (Miami) schools originated the
quinmester idea and had several schools using the plan. School
officials in Utica, Michigan, also made the decision to implement
the Quinmester plan on a pilot basis in 1973.[19]

Flexible Extended School Year Designs

As time progresses, educators seem to acquire a desire to replace
the rigidity found in all phases of the traditional school year program with the flexibility required by modern educational concepts
and the modern society at large. This endeavor has revealed itself
in the most recent attempts to extend the length of the school year.

Some of the extended school year designs have permitted more
options and flexibility for the students, parents, and teachers of
a community than the rotating-term or cycle designs have traditionally permitted. However, a degree of flexibility has been built
into many of the rotating-term or cycle designs by imaginative
and innovative school administrators. Extended school year
designs in the United States which comprise the flexible category
are discussed in the following pages.

Four-One-Four-One-One

A Four-One-Four-One-One experiment project was implemented in Washington High School and in the Franklin Pierce
School in Tacoma, Washington, in 1971. The design of the plan
called for the spreading of student attendance through a 210-day
school year. Student enrollment at any given period of time could
conceivably be some 10 percent less than building capacity. The
extended school year schedule consists of a sixty-four-day fall
semester, a fifth-day schedule of sixteen days, an interim schedule
of twenty days, a spring semester of sixty-four days, a fifth-day
schedule of sixteen days, an interim schedule of twenty days, and
a mini-semester of ten days. According to district officials, the
program was not developed to save money, but to offer alternative
attendance patterns to students and to more fully utilize the school
buildings and facilities.

The sixty-four-day fall and spring semesters are based on a
student's attending school for four days per week over a sixteen-
week period. The two sixteen-day fifth-day terms are composed
of one day per week for each of the sixteen weeks if the student
chooses to attend school five days per week during the fall and
spring semesters. The interim months occur in January and July.

Courses taken during the interim or the mini-semester are taken and completed in the period of time designated for the term.

Any combination of scheduling patterns may be used by students as long as the students attend school for 180 days. Selected academically capable students may attend school for less than 180 days.

The Flexible All-Year Plan

The Flexible All-Year plan was designed to maintain continuous operation of schools year-round. Both the instructional approaches and the time usage in the Flexible All-Year schools are individualized. Schools are conducted in a manner which permits any child or teacher to take a vacation any time of the year for the length of time needed.

With no beginning or ending to the school year in the Flexible All-Year plan, a child is able to enter school whenever the child or parents of the child desire. The child does not have to wait an additional year because of a birth date which occurs a few days too late, as some students have been forced to do in traditional programs. A student does not fail at the end of the school year because there is no end to the school year and no beginning. If illness, conflicts with authority, or vacation causes a student to be out of school at any time, the child returns when appropriate, without the pressure to "catch up" before school is out or fail. The school is expected to be the center of learning, but the community is intended to be the classroom in the Flexible All-Year design.

The Flexible All-Year plan eliminates long summer vacations when the students are dumped on the hot streets with nothing to do. The student does not automatically remain in school twelve years and then get placed on the labor market. Students can choose to leave school when something more important is available to do, or the student may remain in school until something of more interest is found to do.

The Flexible All-Year plan probably will emerge as the plan most capable of meeting the educational needs of a technologically advanced, rapidly changing society because the plan is designed to make optimum use of the time of the members of the educational community. In the long run, such a flexible all-year school plan will likely be the most economically efficient school calendar arrangement as well.[20]

Versions of the Flexible All-Year School plan have been under consideration in two locations: the Wilson Campus School of Mankato State College in Minnesota and the Research-Learning

Center of Clarion State College in Clarion, Pennsylvania. The Flexible All-Year School plan was designed to adapt the educational process to the needs of individual students. The schools are to be conducted continuously throughout the entire year with students entering and leaving at any time desired. The school calendar and course of study for each student are selected by the individual student, and instruction is completely individualized. Each student works at a pace which is comfortable to the student, and acceleration through the academic programs is certainly possible.[21]

Concept Six

Concept Six was arranged on a school calendar which extended the school year beyond nine months for both elementary and secondary levels. The design discards the traditional September-through-May school calendar and replaces such a calendar with one which begins in January and continues through December. When school officials elect to balance the vacation periods selected by students, the Concept Six plan has the effect of producing 50 percent more classroom space.

The Jefferson County, Colorado Concept Six put school buildings and facilities in use 245 days per year and divided the school year into six terms for instructional purposes. Individual students attended classes four of the six terms and chose vacation during the other two terms. Optional attendance for a fifth term was available to students who chose a term for enrichment, remediation, or acceleration purposes, at no added expense to the individual student. Teachers worked the normal 184-day work year but could choose to teach 215 days when student enrollments created the need for additional teachers. Teachers had the traditional holiday vacations, including an extended vacation at Christmas. Six different student entry times have the effect of making the curriculum continuously accessible to students throughout the year and, at the same time, reducing the delay for entry of kindergarten students who reach age five after Labor Day. The multiple entry times for students also make student transfers into and out of the school district easier than was possible in the traditional calendar periods.

A key feature that makes the Concept Six plan desirable to students is the voluntary vacation choice. There are three basic vacation plans in the Jefferson County, Colorado Concept Six. A family may choose any two terms as long as the selections do not seriously alter the balance of enrollment during any one term. Most families vacationed during one of the following three choices:

Vacation Plan A—One vacation from June 27 to August 26 and
the other from January 2 to March 1.

Vacation Plan B—One vacation from August 26 to October 23
and the other from March 1 to April 30.

Vacation Plan C—One vacation from April 30 to June 27 and
the other from October 23 to January 2.

As many as one-third of the students enrolled could be scheduled
for vacation at the same time.[22]

The Continuous Four-Quarter Plan

The Continuous Four-Quarter plan was adopted in Atlanta,
Georgia, to offer year-round educational opportunities and a
more flexible curriculum and to provide a more workable and
relevant educational program. Acceleration, though not the primary purpose, was possible. A lengthened school year was
divided into four equal segments (quarters). Students were given
the option to attend any three quarters during the year—or to attend
all four quarters, if desired. Such a feature distinguished the Continuous Four-Quarter plan from the Quadrimester plan. An essential feature of the Continous Four-Quarter design is that course
offerings are provided which are non-sequential and independent
of each other. A full schedule of all courses and viable alternatives
is to be offered each quarter if the plan is to be successful. By
electing to attend all four quarters, a student could voluntarily
accelerate the educational process. Officials of Atlanta and the
surrounding district were using such a design, not on a pilot or
experimental basis but as the pattern of operation for the school
systems.[23]

Compulsory Extended School Year Designs

The third group of extended school year designs which do not
conform to either of the previous categories is discussed in the
following pages. A choice of attendance and vacation terms is
not a component of these designs; however, opportunities for student acceleration, remediation, enrichment, and increased educational opportunities are presented. Opportunities for teacher
employment beyond the traditional number of school days during
a calendar year are also characteristic of these designs.

The Extended K-Twelve Plan

Unlike the other extended school year plans which are based
upon saving one year out of four, five, or six years of schooling,
the Extended K-Twelve plan limits the savings of time to one year

out of thirteen. The Extended K-Twelve proposal requires the attendance of all pupils through a lengthened school year—providing 204 to 225 instructional days for each of twelve years. The idea is to provide increased educational opportunities for all children with the extra time made available each year through the implementation of the Extended K-Twelve plan.

Teaching emphasis in the Extended K-Twelve plan is placed upon continuous progress from kindergarten through grade six or eight, with no division of the school year taking place until the pupils reach grade seven or nine. The curriculum and related teaching practices in the Extended K-Twelve plan are modified in terms of an organizational pattern based upon the use of trimester, quadrimester, or modified summer school plans. The calendar year saved at the upper grade levels becomes the basis for a reduction in the total school enrollment and the subsequent release of classroom space and teacher time.[24] The Extended K-Twelve plan is actually a combination of several other plans. The most frequently mentioned combination is a continuous school year for the elementary grades combined with a quadrimester or trimester at the secondary level. The proponents of the plan advocate little acceleration at the elementary level; instead, the time is to be used to strengthen skills and broaden educational experiences. The acceleration in academic progress in the Extended K-Twelve plan occurs at the secondary level.[25]

The Quadrimester Plan

In the Quadrimester plan, the school year is divided into four terms of 51 to 55 days. With a small increase in the length of class periods, average learners are expected to complete the course work of two semesters in three quadrimesters. New courses are started immediately after the completion of lower level courses. Enrollments are reduced and classrooms are made available after a transition period of two and one-half years. Financial savings are expected to begin to accrue in the second or third year of operation. Extra educational advantages are available through attendance during extra terms.

While the Quadrimester plan is more expensive than some other plans because of the involvement of additional teachers, the plan still results in the saving of space and dollars after a one- or two-year transition period.[26] In a Quadrimester plan, the school year is approximately 204 to 220 days in length. Like the Trimester, the Quadrimester system has won many advocates at the college level as well as in the public schools.[27]

The Quadrimester plan was designed specifically for acceleration of the educational process. Mandatory student attendance during all terms is an essential feature of the design. With lengthened class periods and a longer school day, students could complete the equivalent work of one year in three quadrimesters, thus allowing time for acceleration and/or enrichment. A modification of the Quadrimester design was implemented on a pilot basis in 1968 at the Park School in Hayward, California. The Quadrimester plan chosen by the Florida legislature was essentially a modified Quadrimester of four, 50-day quarters.[28]

Continuous School Year or Continuous Progress Plan

The Continuous School Year or Continuous Progress plan is based upon a 203- to 216-day calendar which requires flexible school policies and procedures that enable pupils to progress to higher learning activities as soon as the students are ready for new skills and concepts.[29]

One of several variations of the plan provides approximately 200 days of schooling. The Continuous School Year or Continuous Progress plan is highly recommended because it sets the stage for a very flexible and enriched program while leading to potential savings in space. Other variations provide fewer instructional days and possibly a slightly larger increase in school plant capacity.

Recommended Continuous School Year plans have led to the elimination of long, expensive, and wasteful tooling-down processes which started in most schools on or before Memorial Day. Similarly, savings have been realized through elimination of the long tooling-up process which might not be terminated until the end of September or even early October. All educators have not been ready for true continuous progress, but as school officials have moved more schools in the direction of individualized instruction or in the direction of teaching students on the basis of need, the demand for a more flexible school calendar has become evident.[30]

The Continuous School Year Plan, which features a school year of 203 to 216 days with no semester break, proposes a longer school year than was traditionally employed.[31] Pupils complete the work of one grade in the traditional 180 days, then spend the remaining time on the work of the next year.[32]

The Continuous School Year is one of the plans developed by the study group in New York under the direction of George Thomas. The Continuous School Year plan is based upon the idea of continuous progress, and it allows for acceleration through academic work. The plan provides a school year of 210 days, with completion of the work of the regular year in the traditional 180 days. The remaining thirty days are spent on the work of the next grade. The attendance schedule permits pupils to complete seven grades in six years. Pilot programs using the continuous school year have been conducted in the Commack Schools and the School of Human Resources for the Physically Handicapped, both in New York state.[33]

The Extended or Modified Summer School Plan

Most school officials offer strong remedial, make-up, or enrichment programs in summer school. The Modified Summer School plan places emphasis upon a program that enables students to move directly into higher level sequences following courses or programs completed in June. Courses normally taken in a two-semester, 180-day school year are taught in six to eight weeks. Classes meet for daily sessions of three and one-half to four hours. Average learners who attend four or five of the modified summer sessions are supposed to be able to save one year out of six calendar years of schooling.[34] Glencoe, Illinois; Lexington, Kentucky; and Rochester, Minnesota school systems are examples of the successful adoption of the Extended Summer School plan.[35]

The Extended or Modified Summer School plan includes expansion of the conventional summer school. Music appreciation, nature study, swimming instruction, and other nonacademic courses are taught alongside the academics. Attendance during the summer session is optional. Teachers are hired for nine, ten, or eleven months and receive extra compensation for work beyond the basic contracted time. In Glencoe, Illinois, and elsewhere, teachers are employed on a twelve-month basis, which rotates through a five-year cycle. The teachers spend three summers working on curriculum and teaching, one summer studying for an advanced degree, and one summer on vacation. The Extended or Modified Summer Session is probably the most popular of the plans for lengthening the school year.[36]

The Extended Summer School plan is designed to accelerate high school students through the school program by allowing the students to take full-term academic courses for credit during the summer. The Extended or Modified Summer plan as developed by the New York Department of Education permits a student who attends class approximately three and one-half hours a day for seven or eight weeks during the summer to complete the requirements for a single course which normally requires a full year to complete, thus allowing the student to accelerate toward graduation. Another version of the Extended Summer School is similar to the Continuous Four-Quarter or Quinmester plans. The students attend the optional summer term, taking a full range of courses.[37]

Other Variations

Educators in a few school corporations across the country have initiated changes in the traditional school year schedules which encompass the design of year-round or extended school year operations; however, these changes have not been expanded to include summer schedules which provide a complete program of curricular offerings to pupils. For example, the traditional 180-day, nine-month school year has been divided into two of three possible trimesters, three of four possible quarters, etc. These curricular and schedule changes were made in anticipation of the day when state statutes and finances would permit the operation of schools on a year-round or extended school year basis.

The following accounts of various programs are a clear indication of some educationally alert programs as well as one design that is not currently being considered for implementation.

School officials in Logan, Utah, were currently conducting a combination of the Extended or Modified Summer School program. The program was reported to have been in operation since 1960.

Officials in thirty-eight school districts in Texas, or 3.28 percent of the 1,157 school districts in Texas, were experimenting with some form of a Trimester design. Neither detailed data on the Texas programs nor identification of the districts involved were available to be included in the original study, according to officials of the Texas Education Agency. Officials in seventy-one school districts in Georgia were conducting a curriculum organized into Carnegie units taught in blocks of time of two and one-half hours daily for twelve weeks. The seventy-one Georgia school officials have reorganized the traditional school year on a three-quarter basis anticipating implementation of a fourth quarter as soon as funds are available to support the operation. In two of the seventy-one cases, district officials in Georgia are cooperating in a joint effort.

Officials in Houston, Texas, are pilot-testing a Trimester operation in eighteen of the sixty secondary schools in the Houston Independent School District.

Officials in Huntington, West Virginia, reported year-round school operations in one vocational school which was conducted on a forty-five-week school year schedule.

The school officials in Newbury Park, California, reported that the year-round school program scheduled for implementation had been tabled and would be resubmitted for school board approval at such time as increases in the student population warranted such action.

School officials in Salem, Virginia, reported that a continuous school program was to be implemented in the schools of the district in the near future. No detailed information on the program was available to be included in the investigation.

Officials in Shawnee Mission, Kansas, reported having rescheduled the regular school year on a quarter system in anticipation of the time when conditions are suitable to move to a full year quarter program. The suitable time was reported to be when state school financing statutes are changed to make year-round operation of schools feasible.

FOOTNOTES AND REFERENCES

1. Hurnard, John R. "Extending the Scope of the School: Considerations for Reorganizing the School Year." *Oregon School Study Council Bulletin.* College of Education, University of Oregon: Eugene, Oregon, 1972.

2. *Status of the Extended School Year in 1972.* Tallahassee: College of Education, University of Florida, 1972, pp. 5-6.

3. Brodinsky, Ben, Ed. "The Twelve Month School: Six Possible Arrangements." *Education Summary* (October 1, 1967), p. 3.

4. "If You're Interested in the All-Year School" *National Elementary Principal,* 41 (April, 1962), pp. 46-49.

5. *Status of the Extended School Year in 1972. op. cit.*

6. *The Rescheduled School Year.* Research Summary, National Education Association, 1968, p. 10.

7. American Association of School Administrators. *Year-Round Schools.* Washington: The Association, 1960.

8. White, Richard E. "A Board Member Looks at the Extended School Year." *Education,* 88 (March, 1968), pp. 245-248.

9. *Status of the Extended School Year in 1972. op. cit.*

10. Holt, Howard B. "Year-Round Schools and System Shock." *Phi Delta Kappan,* 54 (January, 1973), pp. 310-311.

11. Ernst, Leonard. "The Year-Round School: Faddish or Feasible?" *Nation's Schools,* 88 (November, 1971), pp. 51-56.

12. McLain, John D. "Emerging Plans for Year-Round Education." *Compact,* 4 (December, 1970), pp. 7-8.

13. Allen, James, E., Jr. "All-Year School: Time for a New Look?" *School Management,* 10 (February, 1966), pp. 86-92, 146-156.

14. Brodinsky, *op. cit.*

15. *Status of the Extended School Year in 1972. op. cit.*

16. *Status of the Extended School Year in 1972. op. cit.*

17. Adams, Andrew. "Look Hard at This Year-Round School Plan." *American School Board Journal*, 156 (July, 1968), pp. 11-14, 31.

18. Jensen, George M., *et al.* "Twelve-Month School Year; Panel Discussion." *Compact*, 4 (October, 1970), pp. 28-30.

19. *Status of the Extended School Year in 1972. op. cit.*

20. McLain, John D. "Developing Flexible All-Year Schools." *Educational Leadership*, 28 (February, 1971), pp. 472-475.

21. *Status of the Extended School Year in 1972. op. cit.*

22. White, William D. "Year-Round Education for K-12 Districts." *Phi Delta Kappan*, 54 (January, 1973), pp. 312-313.

23. *Status of the Extended School Year in 1972. op. cit.*

24. Allen, *op. cit.*

25. *Status of the Extended School Year in 1972. op. cit.*

26. Allen, *op. cit.*

27. Brodinsky, *op. cit.*

28. *Status of the Extended School Year in 1972. op. cit.*

29. Allen, *op. cit.*

30. Thomas, George Isaiah. "The Legal and Financial Question." *Compact*, 4 (December, 1970), pp. 9-14.

31. Brodinsky, *op. cit.*

32. "Increased Interest in Longer School Year." *School and Society*, 97 (March, 1969), pp. 155-156.

33. *Status of the Extended School Year in 1972. op. cit.*

34. Allen, *op. cit.*

35. "If You're Interested in the All-Year School." *op. cit.*

36. Brodinsky, *op. cit.*

37. *Status of the Extended School Year in 1972. op. cit.*

Essay Three

THE EXTENDED SCHOOL YEAR:
ISSUES AND ANSWERS

The first recorded indication on the length of the school year was found in the Dorchester, Massachusetts Town Records of 1645. The language of the document required the schoolmaster to begin teaching at seven o'clock in the morning and to dismiss the students at five o'clock in the afternoon for the first seven months of school. During the last five months of the school year (from the eighth month to the end of the twelfth month), the schoolmaster was to begin teaching at eight o'clock in the mornings and to end at four o'clock in the afternoon. Some indication of the length of the school day was discovered in the 1684 rules for the Hopkins Grammar School. The rules required school to be in session from six to eleven o'clock in the morning and from one to five o'clock in the afternoon during the summer months. The closing time was four o'clock in the winter. During the same period of time, school days in Georgia began at sunrise and ended at five o'clock in the afternoon, and the successful schoolmaster taught the entire year.

Throughout the early days of the history of this republic, school district officials often conducted schools for the boys in the winter using male teachers. The boys and male teachers worked on the farms during the summer, and female teachers and girls occupied the schools for educational purposes during the summer months. Apparently this arrangement was the first type of year-round school in the primary or secondary fields of education in this nation. Historically, the idea of an all-year school, according to some writers, can be traced to the year of 1866 when the First Church of Boston reportedly established such a school. The school year was supposedly divided into four quarters of twelve weeks each, with a week of vacation at the end of each twelve-week period.

There can be no "yes" or "no" answers to resolve the issues surrounding the extended school year concept. The contentions of the proponents and the opponents of the concept may both be correct based upon their experience with different extended school year

44

designs or modifications of designs. Each extended school year design was developed, modified, and/or implemented to accomplish specific but different objectives within different school communities, and each design must be evaluated on its own merits in light of the objectives or criteria for which that particular extended school year program was initiated.

The most common issues surrounding the implementation of the extended school year program, as debated by the proponents and opponents of year-round education and affirmatively sanctioned and cited as the most common reasons for implementing extended school year programs in various school corporations, are stated as questions below in decreasing order of importance: (1) Will the implementation of an extended school year program provide better utilization of costly plant facilities which are largely unused or underused during the three months of summer? (2) Will extended school year programs permit improvements and reorganization in the school curriculum? (3) Will extended school year programs prevent the loss of learning by students during the summer vacation? (4) Will the implementation of extended school year programs save a school corporation money by reducing the number of school plant facilities needed to house students? (5) Will extended school year programs make better utilization of the pupils' time during the summer, thereby reducing juvenile delinquency and vandalism? (6) Will extending the school year save money by delaying construction costs and, thus, eliminating the need to ask taxpayers to support additional bond issues? (7) Will the extended school year permit school officials to add enrichment courses to the curriculum? (8) Will an opportunity to attend school year-round reduce the student attrition rate? (9) Will extended school year programs provide a solution to crowded conditions while needed school buildings are being completed? (10) Can teachers mentally, physically, and psychologically endure teaching twelve months per year? (11) Will extended school year programs help disadvantaged students to maintain or acquire acceptable grade level or learning expectations? (12) Can a school corporation save money through implementation of an extended school year program by reducing the number of pupils required to repeat a grade, thereby reducing the school enrollment? (13) Will extended school year programs in a district make teaching more attractive to male teachers and heads of households through greater earning possibilities? (14) Will the extended school year program save money by permitting the acceleration of bright pupils, resulting in a savings of one, two, or three years of schooling in twelve? (15) Will the implementation of extended school year programs force community people to provide needed funds for school construction? (16) Will extended school year attendance improve a student's educational achievement? (17) Will the implementation of an extended school year program provide the needed classroom space to meet increasing student enrollments?

When contemplating an evaluation of the extended school year from which conclusions about the worth, lack of worth, or effects of the concept are to be drawn, the research must be designed or the study population sample must be limited to compensate for the following variations in the organizational structure of different types of extended school year designs and modifications of designs: (1) A majority of the extended school year programs currently in operation in the United States of America do not mandate additional days of employment for teachers nor additional days of school attendance for students during a calendar year. (2) Issues related to juvenile delinquency and vandalism may not be applicable to many elementary schools, many elementary school districts, or many school communities throughout the United States of America. (3) Statistics on the dropout rate of students and the holding power of schools may not be significant in elementary or junior high school situations, depending upon compulsory school attendance regulations within the respective states and the ages of the students enrolled. (4) Data on the average daily attendance rate of students may not be significant in elementary schools, or elementary school communities, and may become meaningless in school corporations with rapid increases in the number of students to be served by the school corporation. (5) Opportunities for student acceleration and remediation in many communities may be kept at a minimum by the design of the extended school year program implemented, state school laws, and/or local school regulations. (6) Data on the effects of extended school year attendance upon the achievement and/or health of students may not be relevant because school attendance for an increased number of days during the calendar year, in most situations, is either by student choice or is not permitted. (7) Academically oriented students may be more inclined to take advantage of voluntary school attendance beyond the traditionally required number of school days in a calendar year. (8) Data on the effects of extended school year attendance upon the retention of cognitive materials by students may be more significant when opportunities are present for all or a portion of the student body in a community to attend school year-round. (9) Comparative data on the cost of conducting extended school year programs may be misleading to the general public unless all variables which affect the cost in each community are presented.

Based upon responses from 131 (89 percent) of 147 school administrators who participated in a nationwide survey of extended school year programs, I have drawn the following conclusions to the age-old contentions of the advocates and opponents of the extended school year concept as to the worth or lack of worth of the concept as a beneficial educational innovation: (1) Teachers (especially male teachers and heads of households) preferred employment for an additional number of school days during the calendar year, if the additional days of employment were accompanied by increased earning opportunities. (2) Resignations and requests for transfers from teachers employed for an extended period of the calendar year occurred no more frequently than requests for transfers and resignations from teachers employed on a conventional school year schedule. (3) Extended school year operations did serve as deterrents to juvenile crime and vandalism. (4) Extending the length of the school year in most school districts did not play a significant role in the decision of students to drop out or to remain in school. (5) A majority of the extended school year operations did not suffer any more than conventional school year programs from a lack of student attendance during any term of the school year. (6) In most school corporations, opportunities for student acceleration and remediation were kept at a minimum by the design of the extended school year program implemented and by state and/or local school regulations. (7) All responding administrators reported that neither the health nor the physical development of students had been noticeably impaired by year-round school attendance. (8) Two-thirds of the administrators surveyed reported that community pressures in the form of defeated bond issues had not caused school officials to decide to implement an extended school year program. The remaining one-third felt that defeated bond issues in the school corporation had left the administrators one alternative—year-round or extended school year operations. (9) Year-round school attendance was reported to have resulted in greater continuity of learning, better retention of cognitive materials, more educational gains, and fewer student failures than school attendance on a conventional school year schedule. (10) Although community opposition to the extended school year concept was considered a difficult problem in many communities, school administrators reported that community opposition decreased in proportion to the length of time the programs continued in operation. (11) Extended school year programs generally did not result in financial savings in the total school budget. In fact, the concept of savings as expressed by proponents of the extended school year concept may have been misleading to the general public. No reduction in the overall amount of current school expenditures should be anticipated as a result of implementing an extended school year program. Proponents of the extended school year concept have based the philosophy of "saving money" upon the probability that extending the length of the school year operations could reduce the increase in the projected amount of additional revenue needed to continue to schedule the schools of a district on a conventional school year basis. (12) A majority of the administrators reported that extended school year attendance resulted in positive gains in academic attainments for students who attended school on an extended school year schedule.

A list of administrative problems confronted by school officials in the implementation and operation of a year-round program was compiled from a review of the literature on extended school year programs; each member of the study population was requested to rank the administrative problems cited in the literature in decreasing order of the magnitude of the problem in the respective school district.

The school officials were also requested to indicate with an "X" the administrative problems listed on the instrument that were not problems in the respective districts. Space was allotted for responding officials to add major problems faced in conducting a year-round or extended school year program which were not found in the predetermined list included in the survey form.

Among the administrative problems generally associated with extended school year operations as voiced by school administrators, in decreasing order of response frequencies, are the following: (1) lack of time for teachers involved in the program to attend school for professional growth; (2) conflicts between schedules of schools conducted on extended or year-round plans and those conducted on a traditional basis; (3) community opposition; (4) inadequate time for maintenance, renovation, clean-up work, and repairs; (5) teacher opposition; (6) inadequate funds for conducting extended sessions; (7) low student attendance rates during the summer months; (8) student opposition; (9) scheduling members of the same family into school during the same term; (10) scheduling all interested student participants into extracurricular activities during the terms when the activities are in session; (11) scheduling an equal number of boys and girls into school each term; (12) communicating with parents and teachers on the extended school year concept; (13) development of intersession curriculum; (14) development of extended school year programs suited to the needs of the community; (15) added operational costs; (16) no vacation time for administrators; (17) internal school scheduling; (18) community involvement in planning extended school year programs; (19) communication of the extended school year concept and philosophies to the school corporation; (20) distribution of students to maintain a suitable balance of class size among the attendance groups; (21) staff involvement in planning extended school year programs; (22) educating parents to the extended school year philosophy; (23) student record keeping; (24) lack of materials for new curriculum; and (25) recruitment of staff for summer employment (see Appendix A).

When school administrators were requested to assign a rank (the rank of one represented the most difficult problems of the school district) to each administrative problem according to the difficulty level of the problem in the respective school districts the following administrative problems were ranked and are listed below, based upon the frequency with which the rank of *one* was assigned to the problem. The administrative problems that did not receive rankings of number one are listed in sequence in the preceding paragraph and are not included in the list which follows: (1) inadequate funds for operating extended session; (2) community opposition; (3) teacher opposition; (4) conflicts between schedules of schools conducted on extended or year-round schedule and schools on traditional schedule; (5) scheduling members of the same family in school during same term; (6) lack of time for teachers involved in program to attend school and gain professional growth; (7) scheduling equal number of boys and girls into school each term; (8) low attendance rate during summer months; (9) development of extended school year program suited to needs of the community; (10) student opposition; (11) staff involvement in planning extended year program; (12) district understanding of extended year program; (13) distribution of students to maintain a suitable balance of class size among the four attendance groups; (14) development of intersession curriculum; (15) no vacation time for administrators; (16) internal school scheduling; and (17) recruitment of staff for summer work.

EFFECTS OF EXTENDED SCHOOL
YEAR OPERATIONS

For more than three-quarters of a century, advocates and opponents of the extended school year or year-round school concept in education have debated the pros and cons of issues related to the effects of extending the school year operations. The debates were focused upon those teachers and students who were involved in school routines for a number of days during a calendar year which exceeded the traditional number of calendar days for school operation. Research into the effects of year-round or extended school year operations, since the decade of the 1930's, has been minimal and inconclusive and has failed to resolve the contentions of the proponents or the opponents as to the strengths and/or weaknesses of the concept. Much of the vast amount of literature related to the effects of extended school year or year-round school operations has been conjectural and seemed to have embraced the writers' biases which were, in many cases, based upon analyses of hypothetical extended school year operations.

Advocates of extending the length of the school year have argued that teachers (especially male teachers and heads of households) preferred school employment for an additional number of school days during the calendar year because of increased earning possibilities. Extended school year advocates contend that the lengths of the conventional school year have caused teachers to be part-time employees who felt alienated toward many aspects of the local communities in which they were employed. Teachers have been left without employment for two or three months of the calendar year and have been forced to seek other permanent employment or to seek part-time employment to supplement their teaching salaries. Proponents of the extended school year concept believe that teachers should be employed on a twelve-month basis with a one-month paid vacation each year. However, proponents and opponents of the extended school year concept agree that the physical and emotional strain of teaching twelve months per year may be excessive for some teachers. Other teachers may find a three-month vacation every two or three years adequate for personal recuperation and rejuvenation. A consensus of opinion among proponents of extended school year operations is that year-round employment would improve the professional status of teachers, give teachers greater financial security, and bring benefits to the community through greater teacher involvement and better student-teacher relationships.

Opponents of the extended school year concept contend that school people reserve their summers for rest, recuperation, travel, advanced study, evaluation of past programs, preparation for future programs, and neglected family living. Although, in the opinion of the opponent, teaching is a rewarding, challenging, and inspiring profession, it is also an exhausting profession which chips away at teacher morale. Nervous exhaustion builds up while teaching, and vacations are a welcomed sight for thousands of teachers around the world. Teaching cannot be compared to office work; teachers need vacations from school routines—long vacations. Opponents of the extended school year concept believe that a longer school year is likely to hasten the defection of teachers from the teaching profession and that the day the summer vacations from school are eliminated teachers will reluctantly resign or retire from teaching.

Another contention of the extended school year advocates is that extended school year operations could reduce the student attrition rates and increase the holding power of the schools. The reduced attrition rates among students and the increased holding power of the schools were to be accomplished through opportunities for student acceleration and remediation during the additional term or terms of the school year. By taking advantage of acceleration opportunities, students of average or above average intelligence could fulfill the graduation requirements of the state and/or local school district before reaching the minimum school dropout age permitted by law. According to advocates of the extended school year concept, acceleration of student progress through the grades could release needed classroom space and possibly postpone the need to construct new school housing facilities in many communities. Acceleration could also reduce the need for increased numbers of teachers and custodial employees and reduce school transportation costs. Acceleration of the academic process would permit young people to enter professional schools and colleges at an early age. This early entrance would permit early graduation from school and provide additional years of gainful employment in professions which normally require many years of academic preparation. Through remedial opportunities, reluctant learners could remove deficiencies which were acquired during one term of a school year by attending school for an additional term of the same school year. The practice of repeating a grade would disappear, and students who normally experienced school failures could graduate from high school in the traditionally expected number of years.

Opponents of the extended school year concept have argued that acceleration of students through the grades could result in the graduation of elementary students who are too immature for high school work; and, as a result, a large portion of the educational gains previously acquired by such students through extended school year attendance would be lost.

Spokesmen for the advocates of year-round or extended school year operations have reported a definite relationship between school vacation periods and the peak periods of juvenile delinquency and vandalism in a community. The most critical periods of juvenile delinquency and vandalism were reported to have occurred during the Easter, Christmas, and summer vacation periods from school. Delinquency and vandalism were reported to have come to an abrupt decrease when students returned to school. These contentions of the extended school year proponents have been supported by data in the records of juvenile court judges and data in police records of juvenile arrests. Year-round school operations with opportunities for year-round student attendance is viewed by advocates of the concept as a deterrent to juvenile crime.

During the year-round school experiments of the 1920's and 1930's, school officials found that the average daily attendance rate for students enrolled in school for an additional period of the calendar year was slightly higher than the average daily attendance rate for students enrolled in school programs of conventional school year lengths. Administrators of these early extended school year programs also found that the average daily attendance rate for students during the summer term of the extended school year represented the highest average daily attendance rate for students during any of the school terms of the calendar year. Opponents of the extended school year concept have argued that year-round school operations (and especially the summer terms) would suffer from a lack of attendance by students.

Research into the gains and losses in student achievement and retention of cognitive data during the long summer vacation has been mixed and inconclusive. Some writers have reported a loss in the level of cognitive retention by students during the long vacation periods from school, while other writers have reported slight gains or no significant difference in student cognitive development during the traditional summer vacation periods from school. Some writers have also reported that three or four months of teaching and learning during each subsequent school year were required to regain the losses which occurred in student cognitive retention during the long summer vacation periods. A general consensus among year-round or extended school year advocates is that a slight loss occurs in the retention of cognitive skills by students during the long summer vacation from school. The advocates contend that year-round school attendance by students would result in a steady gain in a student's cognitive development rather than a loss. Children retain learning much better if the opportunities are present for continued education throughout the calendar year.

Opponents of the extended school year concept have argued that extended school year or year-round school attendance would have a detrimental effect upon the health of students. This theory of the extended school year opponents is based upon the philosophy that students need direct sunlight, fresh air, and vigorous exercise for adequate physical development. Various writers have attributed statements to the opponents of the extended school year concept which conclude that students need long vacations from school routines. The writers contend that the mental and physical strain of schooling upon the student's body produces nervous fatigue which may result in neurosis in adult life.

Advocates of the extended school year concept have refuted the contentions of the opponents and have reported that carefully designed research has not presented a single observation which would justify the conclusions that either the health or growth of a pupil is impaired by attending school year-round. The health of students who attended school for an additional number of days during the calendar year has been reported to be as good, if not better, than the health of students who attended school on a traditional school year schedule. The school is a wholesome atmosphere for many students when compared to their homes or the streets. This is especially true in congested city areas where homes are poorly ventilated and extremely hot during the summer months. Physicians with national prominence have sanctioned these contentions of the extended school year advocates.

A resolution to the contentions of the proponents and opponents of the extended school year concept can only be achieved through carefully designed research into the effects and implications of the concept. Attempts to design research on the extended school year that will isolate and control the many variables, provide internal and external validity, and resolve the issues concerning the effects and implications of the extended school year concept on a comparative basis may be a difficult task. Because of the development of many different types of extended school year designs and modification of existing designs, there is no common set of criteria to which an evaluation of all extended school year programs can be subjected. The same situation is equally paramount from school district to school district even when the extended school year design implemented appears to be the same or similar based upon labels and structure. General statements (such as the contentions attributed to the opponents and advocates of the extended school year or year-round school concept in this article) related to the effects, implications, advantages, and disadvantages of the extended school year concept are no longer applicable to all extended school year or year-round school operations. Each extended school year design, modification, or variation of a design was developed, modified, selected, and/or implemented to accomplish specific but different objectives within different school communities; and each design or modification of a design must be evaluated in light of the objectives or criteria for which that particular extended school year program was initiated.

In a nationwide survey of extended school year programs, school administrators were requested to respond to the issues previously raised throughout this book concerning the effects of the extended school year concept. The responses from the administrators were to be based upon their experience and factual knowledge of the effects of the extended school year operations in their respective school corporations. These administrators represented 63 percent of the entire study population of seventy-nine extended school year operations which were actully in existence in the United States of America at the time of this investigation.

According to a majority of the responses from administrators of extended school year programs, male teachers and heads of households definitely preferred employment for an extended number of days during the calendar year. This was especially true when the design of the extended school year program permitted additional school days of employment for teachers during the calendar year accompanied by increased earning opportunities.

Based upon the reports of 92 percent of the responding administrators, teacher resignations and requests for transfers from teachers employed for an extended period of the calendar year occurred no more frequently than requests for transfers and resignations from teachers employed on a conventional school year schedule. Eight percent of the responding officials reported an increase in teacher resignations and requests for transfers from teachers employed on an extended school year contract.

When comparing the attrition rate of students enrolled in extended school year programs with the attrition rate of students enrolled in the same school or schools before the program was implemented, 72 percent of the responding officials reported that the dropout rate among the two groups of students had remained unchanged. Twenty-four percent reported a decrease in the student attrition rate among the extended school year students since the program was implemented in the schools. Only one official reported an increase in the student dropout rate in the extended school year program since the extended school year program was implemented; however, factors not related to extending the school year caused the increase in this particular school. In a comparison of the dropout rate of students currently enrolled in extended school year programs with the dropout rate of students currently enrolled in conventional school year programs, 89 percent of the responding officials reported no apparent difference in the dropout rate of the two school groups. Eleven percent reported the student dropout rate in conventional schools to be higher than the student dropout rate in extended school year schools. It is logical to assume that the implementation of the extended school year program in most districts has not played a significant role in the decision of students to drop out or remain in school; however, the design of the extended school year program may have an effect upon the dropout data.

Fifty-four percent of the responding officials reported that the current average daily attendance rate for students enrolled in the extended school year program was higher than the average daily attendance rate of students enrolled in the same school before the program was implemented. Forty-two percent reported that the average daily attendance rate for students currently enrolled in the extended school year program remained about the same as the average daily attendance rate of students in the same school before the program was implemented. Only one administrator reported that the average daily attendance rate of students in the school converted to extended school year operation was lower after implementation of the extended school year program. When comparing the average daily attendance rate of students currently enrolled in extended school year programs with the average daily attendance rate of students currently enrolled in conventional schools, 52 percent of the responding officials reported that there was no noticeable difference in the average daily attendance rates of the two groups of students. Forty-three percent reported higher average daily attendance rates for students currently enrolled in extended school year programs, and one official reported higher average daily attendance rates for students enrolled in conventional programs. The average daily attendance rates for students during the summer term of the extended school year program as compared to the average daily attendance rates for students during other terms of the extended school year were reported by 53 percent of the responding officials to have indicated no obvious difference in the average daily attendance rates of students during the summer months. Thirty-eight percent reported a lower average daily attendance rate for students during the summer months, and 9 percent reported the average daily attendance rate of students during the summer to be higher than the average daily attendance rate for students during other terms of the extended school year. Based upon these responses, which were influenced by the design of the extended school year programs in operation in a particular school corporation, a majority of the extended school year operations do not suffer any more than conventional school year programs from a lack of student attendance during any term of the school year; but in a few cases conventional school year programs seem to have a slight edge on extended school year programs in the average daily attendance rate of students.

According to responses from school administrators, students had been permitted to avoid repeating a course by using the additional term or terms of the extended school year for remediation and make-up opportunities in six school corporations. In eleven school corporations, students had been permitted to accelerate their academic progress by one year through school attendance for an additional school term. In most school corporations, opportunities for student acceleration and remediation were kept at a minimum by the design of the extended school year program implemented and by state and local school regulations. Many of the extended school year programs currently in operation were implemented to release classroom space in densely populated school buildings, not to permit year-round educational opportunities for larger numbers of the student population.

One-hundred percent of the responding officials reported that the health and physical development of students had not been noticeably impaired by extended school year attendance.

Sixty-two and one-half percent of the responding administrators reported that, as measured by standardized test results and grade reports, extended school year attendance had had a positive effect upon the academic achievement of the enrolled students. Thirty-seven and one-half percent reported that the academic achievement of students remained unchanged in spite of extended school year attendance; however, no administrator reported a loss in academic attainment for students while attending extended school year programs. In comparing students of the same sex, age, and similar I.Q. scores who currently attended extended school year programs with similar students who currently attended school on a conventional schedule, 56 percent of the responding officials reported positive gains in achievement for the extended school year students. Forty-four percent reported no noticeable gains in achievement for extended school year students. When comparing educational gains for extended school year students of the same age, sex, and I.Q. with students of similar age and sex but higher I.Q. scores who attended school on a conventional basis, 50 percent of the responding officials reported no gains for the extended school year students, and 50 percent reported that students enrolled in extended school year programs had slight educational gains on similar students with higher I.Q. scores.

Year-round school attendance was reported to have resulted in greater continuity of learning, better retention of cognitive materials, positive gains in educational benefits, and fewer student failures than school attendance on a conventional school year schedule.

Extended school year programs generally did not result in financial savings in the total school budget. In fact, the concept of savings as expressed by proponents of the extended school year concept could have been misleading to the general public. No reduction in the overall amount of current school expenditures should be anticipated as a result of implementing an extended school year program. Proponents of the extended school year concept have based the philosophy of "saving money" upon the probability that extending the length of the school year operations could reduce the increase in the projected amount of additional revenue needed to continue to schedule the schools of a district on a conventional school year basis.

Essay Five

THE LENGTHENED SCHOOL YEAR
AND JUVENILE CRIME

Although juvenile crimes occur throughout each calendar year, the school vacation periods and the peak periods of juvenile delinquency are closely related. When schools are closed and hundreds of students are set free with nothing constructive to occupy their minds, trouble begins, and juvenile arrests are recorded more frequently. Educators report, and records of police arrests of juvenile offenders sanction the fact, that the high point of juvenile crime comes during the Easter, Christmas, spring, and summer vacation periods from school—times when students are neither mentally nor physically engaged in the wholesome, supervised activities provided by school attendance. After the holiday periods, students return to school, and there is an abrupt decrease in the number of juvenile crimes committed. The truth of the previous assertions has been repeatedly documented and reported during the past three-quarters of a century; yet, the length of our school year continues to stand as a monument to a bygone agrarian life and as an opportunity for increased juvenile crime in America.

Without the implementation of a year-round school program, students are left to shift for themselves and to run the streets from two and one-half to three months every summer. Particularly in cities, a great deal of time is spent in playing in the streets and alleys. The conditions of the environment—congested, noisy and hot streets and everywhere temptations to explore, discover, and misbehave—cause the juvenile courts to be clogged every morning with young offenders. Extending the length of the school year invites the young people to come off the streets during the summer into a place better adapted to their nature and needs. In many cases, students left unsupervised throughout the day is not good; yet, the situation often exists during the vacation periods from school. Many parents have neither the time, the inclination, nor the training to properly supervise the play activities of children throughout the summer. The implication is that long vacation periods from school should be eliminated so that school officials may supervise juvenile recreational activities during vacations and keep a closer check on the outside influences that are detrimental to the lives of the young.

Many students are not able financially to take trips during the vacation periods; few are financially able to go to summer camp; thus, juvenile crime begins to rise from idle minds. In spite of all the teaching on idle hands—the Koran, the Torah, the Talmud, and the Holy Bible—the street environment of the cities continues to educate children for hospital beds, asylums, jails, and penitentiaries. During this time, the great school buildings provide a job for a janitor or two and eat, like a moth, a hole of fixed charges into the school budget which the taxpayers must ultimately pay. The shops and gymnasiums; the cool classrooms with beautiful pictures, movie machines, books, and chalkboards; and windows which would breed flowers but do not, all stand idle, or at best are used for an hour or two each day.

Proponents of year-round education believe that extending the length of the school year could substantially reduce juvenile delinquency. The extent of the reduction in the delinquency rate among students of a school corporation will be directly affected by the type of extended school year design implemented in the district. If the implemented extended school year design requires compulsory or mandatory school attendance year-round by all school-age students of the district, the juvenile crime rate will be reduced significantly. If the implemented extended school year design requires school attendance on a rotating-term or cycle basis, the juvenile crime rate should be reduced by the percentage of the student population enrolled in school each term of the school year; or the juvenile crime rate should be in proportion to the season of the school year and the number of students on vacation from school each school term of the calendar year. If the extended school year program requires school attendance by all students for a period of time equal to the length of the conventional or traditional school year and permits school attendance on an optional basis for an additional term or terms of the school year, the juvenile crime rate may not be significantly altered. Attending school for an extended period of the calendar year may not be an attractive proposition for students who live in environments which tend to breed juvenile criminals.

For the unfortunate child to whom vacation means aimless loafing on the streets, there should be some form of extended school year operations, possibly compulsory and supported by the state. Parents are not always able to furnish suitable occupations or recreation for the child during vacation periods. Year-round schools are a good means of showing common sense in the use of available time and resources. Year-round schools are progress with which fine leadership can face a new dawn in education. Wouldn't it be a comforting feeling to know that your children are under the supervision of some responsible agency while you work all day?

If the United States of America would apply a portion of the current cost of juvenile crime to the schools' operating costs, and if the school curriculum were flexible with many activity offerings, many juvenile criminal cases would be kept off the police record books. Many educators are in complete agreement with the theory of permitting school buildings, playgrounds, gymnasiums, libraries, and auditoriums to remain open to children for recreational purposes seven days and nights each week and 365 days and nights each year. Such a program would entail immediate expenses to taxpayers but would also result in savings because the costs of utilizing buildings for recreational purposes are much cheaper than to eventually build additional prisons and reformatories to rehabilitate youngsters who were forced to seek recreation in questionable places.

The current economic conditions in this country are causing the public to react negatively toward increases in taxation despite the most noble of causes, and school officials are being forced to examine and reexamine numerous extended or year-round school programs as alternatives to higher taxes for school operations, constructions, and/or renovations. As more and more school officials are forced to implement year-round school programs, as a by-product, it is quite possible that we will reap a decrease in juvenile crime and in the amount of public revenue spent on crime in general. After all, many adult criminals started their lives of crime as juvenile offenders. If the juvenile delinquents had been rehabilitated, in many cases, the adult criminal would not have existed. As school officials are forced to implement extended school year programs and as decreases in the amount of public funds spent on juvenile and adult crime are realized, the savings on crime should be directed toward keeping the schools open every day and night in the year. According to most authorities and prognosticators on the lengthened school year and juvenile crime, there would still be huge savings in public funds beyond those needed to conduct the lengthened school year, and great social benefits would accrue to society in the form of a reduced criminal element.

Although juvenile crime is constantly on the rise, the implementation of a lengthened school year would help prevent the crimes, and year-round school operations also have the potential to add to the creative expression of the individual. Pupils may seldom have time to pursue many interests because the short, traditional-length school term is too structured. A longer school term could provide each student the opportunity to do remedial work, accelerate the academic process, and follow many unexplored interests.

An extended school year program could keep students busy in a wholesome, purposeful situation which, through development of skills, sportsmanship, and cooperative competition, would ultimately lead to a reduction in juvenile delinquency and adult crime.

Summer vacation schools were first attempted as a solution to juvenile crime. One of the most encouraging of all the summer programs, the Florida Summer Enrichment Program of the 1950's, resulted in an actual decrease in juvenile delinquency during the summer months when, for the country as a whole, delinquency increased sharply. The Continuous Four-Quarter extended school year design currently in operation in Fulton County (Atlanta), Georgia, is believed to be serving as a possible deterrent to juvenile crime.

In a nationwide survey of seventy-nine school corporations in which extended school year or year-round programs were operational or were contemplated for operation in the U.S.A., fifty (63 percent) of the responding school officials representing the operational extended school year population reported the following responses to four questions related to the length of the school year and the juvenile crime rates in their respective school districts. Sixty percent of the responding school officials reported a decrease in delinquency rate among students who were currently enrolled in extended school year programs as compared to the delinquency rate among students who attended the same schools before the extended school year program was implemented. Thirty-three percent of the responding officials reported that no change was apparent in the delinquency rate among students currently enrolled in extended school year programs as compared to students enrolled in the same school prior to implementation of the extended school year program. Seven percent reported an increase in the delinquency rate among students currently enrolled in the extended school year programs but cited reasons other than extending the length of the school year as a major cause of the increase.

Fifty-four percent of the responding school administrators reported no apparent difference in the delinquency rate among students currently enrolled in extended school year programs and the rate among students currently enrolled in conventional school year programs. Seventeen percent reported the current delinquency rate to be lower among students enrolled in extended school year programs. Thirteen percent reported that the requested data were not applicable to their elementary extended school year programs. Eight percent reported a lower delinquency rate among students currently enrolled in traditional school year programs. Four percent reported that a response would depend upon the area of the city in question, and four percent reported that all students of the district were enrolled in extended school year programs, which eliminated the possibility of a comparison.

Fifty-one percent of the responding school officials reported a decrease in the amount of vandalism which occurred in schools conducted on an extended school year basis when compared to the vandalism rate in the same schools prior to the implementation of the extended school year program. Forty-three percent of the responding school administrators reported that no apparent change had occurred in the rate of vandalism among students enrolled in the extended school year programs since the programs were implemented. Six percent reported that the requested data were not applicable to the local district situation.

Forty-four percent of the responding school officials reported no apparent difference in the vandalism rate among students currently enrolled in schools conducted on an extended school year schedule and the vandalism rate among students currently enrolled in conventional school year programs. Thirty-three percent reported that more vandalism occurred in schools conducted on a traditional school year schedule than in schools currently conducted on an extended school year schedule. Eleven percent reported that the requested data were not applicable to the local elementary school situation. Six percent reported that all schools were conducted on an extended school year basis, which eliminated schools scheduled on a conventional basis with which to make a comparison. Three percent reported less vandalism in the traditional schools, and three percent reported that a response depended upon the area of the city under consideration.

Some may wish to question the relationship between the rate of juvenile delinquency and the school vacation periods. The contention is that the festive activities of the Christmas and Easter seasons of the year and the decorative shop displays have greater influence upon a child's desire to commit crime than the mere fact that the child is on vacation from school. If a comparison is made between the juvenile crime rates of the Christmas and Easter vacation periods from school and the juvenile crime rate of school vacation periods during other seasons of the year, the results of the investigation will consistently support the validity in the previous assertion; however, such results do not account for the increased rate in juvenile crime during school vacation periods at times other than Christmas and Easter when compared to the periods of regular school attendance.

If "an idle mind is the devil's workshop," it is time that society encourage and demand that the school corporations lease the devil's workshops year-round and conduct constructive, character-building programs in such vacant spaces. The schools must once again share the challenge with the parents to mold and shape the character of students, which ultimately shapes society. With the lack of home industries and a lack of agrarian industries of the early 1900's to occupy the child's time, the functions of the school cannot be continued on a part-time basis but must be conducted year-round to accommodate the increasing amounts of leisure time found on the students' hands. As a result, many would-be juvenile offenders who also might become adult criminals will become pillars of respectability as adult leaders in society.

FOOTNOTES AND REFERENCES

Adams, Velma A. "The Extended School Year: A Status Report." *School Management* (June, 1970), 15.

"All Year School." *Elementary School Journal,* 30 (October, 1929), 83-84.

"All-Year Schools One Way of Reducing Crime." *Nation's Schools,* 4 (August, 1929), 34.

Clifford, J. M. "The Wasteful School Year." *American School Board Journal,* 117 (September, 1948), 24.

"Freedom of the Street Versus All-Year School." *Nation's Schools,* 4 (September, 1929), 74-75.

Hartsell, Horace C. "The Twelve-Month School." *Bulletin of the National Association of Secondary School Principals,* 37 (December, 1953), 18-33.

"Increased Interest in Longer School Year." *School and Society,* 97 (March, 1969), 155-156.

Lane, Elias N. "The All-Year School—Its Origin and Development." *Nation's Schools,* 9 (March, 1932), 49-52.

Maynard, Zollie M., and Thomas D. Bailey. "Summer School with a Difference." *Journal of the National Education Association*, 46 (May, 1957), 297-299.

Peterson, Robert. "The Twelve-Month School." *The American School Board Journal*, 110 (May, 1945), 38-40.

Roe, W. A. "The All-Year School." *Bulletin of the Department of Elementary School Principals*, 6 (October, 1926), 10-22.

Essay Six

EXTENDED SCHOOL YEAR DESIGNS FOR BUILDINGS AND FACULTY VERSUS THOSE FOR PUPIL PROGRESS

In a national publication in March, 1974, I identified the various types of extended school year or year-round school designs currently in operation in the U.S.A. Since that time, I have been bombarded with requests from school administrators across the country to categorize those identified school year designs into the following categories: (1) designs for the benefit of buildings and faculty, and (2) designs for the benefit of student educational progress.

Because of the vast amount of publicity given the rotating-term or cycle extended school year designs, many school administrators are vaguely aware of the existence of year-round or extended school year programs which permit and/or mandate school attendance for all or a portion of the student population in a school corporation on an extended school year basis. Many administrators have the conception that only rotating-term or cycle extended school year designs exist, or the administrators are unable to distinguish by title the rotating-term or cycle designs from extended school year or year-round programs which require and/or permit students to attend school for more days during the calendar year than they traditionally have been permitted to attend.

Because of the development of many different types of extended school year designs and because of modifications in existing designs in various school corporations, I am not certain that a clear-cut, categorical differentiation (extended school year designs for buildings and faculty versus extended school year designs for pupils) is possible.

Any extended school year design currently in existence could financially benefit all or a portion of the faculty in a school community through extended school year employment, depending upon the needs and desires found within a given community. All extended school year designs could release classroom space and facilities based upon the attendance patterns of students in a community. The issue becomes how much space will be released by implementing a particular extended school year design and how soon the space will be released. Any opportunities for student acceleration or remediation of the academic process through extended school year attendance will result in early graduation from school for some students, thereby releasing classroom space. These opportunities for acceleration and remediation should provide a situation wherein students will be graduating from school at a faster rate than they enter, thereby releasing classroom space.

Any extended school year program must benefit students to some degree. A rotating-term or cycle design will release varying amounts of crowded classroom space, thereby providing an atmosphere more conducive to student learning. Other extended school year designs which require and/or permit extended school year attendance for all students or a portion of the student body in a community will provide opportunities for students to accelerate, remediate, or enrich the educational process.

There are extended school year programs (rotating-term or cycle) in existence in the U.S.A. which provide year-round utilization of school buildings and facilities and year-round employment for all or a portion of the faculty. Although different rotating-term or cycle designs provide opportunities for varying percentages of the student population to attend school throughout the calendar year, the remaining percentage of the student body is on vacation from school throughout each segment of the calendar year. These designs *usually* do not permit individual students to attend school for a number of calendar days to exceed the number of days of school attendance traditionally permitted in a school district.

Despite the previous discourse, extended school year designs currently in operation which comprise the "for buildings and faculty" category are as follows: (1) the Forty-Five—Fifteen or the Nine-Three; (2) the Rotating Trimester; (3) the Twelve-Four Trimester or the Sixty-Twenty; (4) the Rotating Four-Quarter; and (5) any other rotating-term or cycle design.

There are also extended school year designs currently in operation in the U.S.A. which mandate extended school year attendance for all students of the district (204-225 days). There are other extended school year designs currently in operation which provide opportunities for students to attend school year-round or for an additional number of days during the calendar year, and school officials strongly encourage students to take advantage of those opportunities. Designs which comprise the "for students" category are as follows: (1) The Quinmester or the Pentamester (ESY attendance encouraged); (2) the Quadrimester (204-220 days—attendance mandated for all participating students); (3) the Continuous Four-Quarter (ESY attendance encouraged); (4) Concept Six (ESY attendance encouraged); (5) the Flexible All-Year (ESY attendance encouraged); (6) the Extended K-Twelve (204-225 days—attendance mandated for all participating students); (7) the Four-One-Four-One-One (ESY attendance encouraged); and (8) the Continuous School Year (ESY attendance strongly encouraged).

Where more than one extended school year design has been placed beside the same number in the above listings, the extended school year designs are considered to be quite similar. In view of the previous statement, one may conclude that distinctions in extended school year programs by title only serve to confuse and add to the lack of concept development in education; but these title distinctions are very real and important to school officials in communities where the title differences exist. It is my contention that the wishes of school officials in these communities should be honored.

Essay Seven

VARIATIONS IN THE "FORTY-FIVE—FIFTEEN" EXTENDED SCHOOL YEAR DESIGN

The Forty-Five—Fifteen plan, developed and implemented as the Nine-Three (weeks of attendance and vacation) in St. Charles, Missouri, in 1969, and implemented as the Forty-Five—Fifteen (days of attendance and vacation) in Lockport, Illinois, in 1970, has been gaining acceptance across the country by community people and school officials. The Forty-Five—Fifteen design or variations of the design represent 47 percent of the seventy-nine extended school year programs currently in operation in the country . The number of Forty-Five—Fifteen designs and the states in which the designs are currently in operation have been tabulated and are presented in the following table.

CURRENTLY OPERATING FORTY-FIVE—FIFTEEN EXTENDED
SCHOOL YEAR DESIGNS

STATE	NUMBER OF SCHOOL CORPORATIONS	PERCENTAGE OF TOTAL
Arizona	5	13.51
California	18	48.65
Colorado	1	2.70
Florida	1	2.70
Illinois	2	5.41
Michigan	1	2.70
Missouri (Nine-Three)	1	2.70
Minnesota	1	2.70
Ohio	1	2.70
Oregon	2	5.41
North Carolina	1	2.70
Vermont	1	2.70
Virginia	2	5.41
TOTAL	37	99.99

The Forty-Five—Fifteen was originally designed to place school buildings on year-round operation with four equally distributed groups of students, comprising the entire school building population, scheduled to attend school on a rotating basis. The plan did not provide school attendance opportunities for an extended number of school days during the calendar year for any student. Each student was to attend school for a number of days during the calendar year equal to the attendance period of the conventional school year schedule. The Forty-Five—Fifteen was not designed to permit student acceleration through the grades but to provide year-round utilization of available classroom space. The purpose of the design was to reduce or eliminate the need to invest large sums of additional public funds into school construction and, at the same time, provide adequate classroom space for all students of the district. In recent years, in addition to the rotating-term or cycle Forty-Five—Fifteen design, the plan has been modified to include aspects of the more flexible extended school year designs.

One variation of the Forty-Five—Fifteen design permits all students to attend school for four forty-five day terms. Each term is followed by fifteen-day intersession courses on an optional attendance basis. In various school districts, the intersession courses permit opportunities for student acceleration, remediation, or enrichment. This variation of the Forty-Five—Fifteen design permits year-round employment for all or a percentage of the teaching staff, depending upon the demands resulting from student enrollment during the intersession terms.

Another variation of the Forty-Five—Fifteen design permits all students to attend school for four forty-five day terms, but each term is followed by fifteen-day vacation periods for all students. This variation of the Forty-Five—Fifteen permits year-round employment for teachers, or teachers may observe the same attendance and vacation periods as students. In some school corporations, the fifteen-day student vacation periods are not vacation periods for teachers. Teachers are paid year-round, and the student vacation periods are used by teachers for parent-teacher conferences, in-service workshops and conferences, and teacher planning and preparation.

It would be interesting to see school officials modify and implement the Sixty-Twenty rotating-term or cycle design on the basis wherein all students attend school at the same time and take vacation from school during the same time period. If the Sixty-Twenty were implemented on the first of September in any given year, there would result a one-month Christmas vacation in December, a one-month spring vacation in April, and a one-month summer vacation in August.

Because the Nine-Three and the Forty-Five—Fifteen are two strikingly similar modifications of the staggered or rotating four-quarter year-round school design, many educators, interested in the year-round education movement, have been baffled since 1970 over the inability to differentiate between the operational procedures of the two designs.

The Nine-Three and the Forty-Five—Fifteen were developed and implemented to place school buildings into operation year-round. Neither plan was originally designed to increase the actual number of days of school attendance for students within a twelve-month period nor to permit opportunities for students to accelerate, remediate, or enrich the academic process. The designs are meant to provide year-round utilization of available classroom space and facilities and to reduce or eliminate the need to invest huge sums of additional public funds into capital outlay projects. This is to be accomplished by year-round operation of existing school buildings and by permitting only three-fourths of the student population to be housed in those existing school buildings at any given time within a twelve-month period.

The Nine-Three and the Forty-Five—Fifteen require the division of the student population into four "equal" groups. Although the main point in the division of students is to acquire four equal size groups of students in number, each of the four student groups should be assembled in a manner to derive equal representation from the racial composition of the community, the various student age groups, and both sex groups, and to distribute student mental capabilities equally among each of the four student groups.

Both designs can accommodate numerous variations in employment and vacation schedules for teachers, depending upon the needs and desires of the individual teacher and the needs and desires of the school community. Four possible teacher employment and vacation options are as follows: (1) to accept employment during any four of the five rotating-cycle terms and vacation during any one of the five terms; (2) to accept year-round employment with a minimum number of vacation days; (3) to accept employment and vacation patterns which coincide with student attendance and vacation patterns in any operational variation of the two designs; and (4) to contract services for the traditional school year or the equivalent number of days.

In spite of the many apparent similarities, slight differences do exist between the Nine-Three and the Forty-Five—Fifteen operations. In recent years, in addition to the five-term (225 days) rotating-cycle designs previously discussed, the Forty-Five—Fifteen rescheduled school year design has been modified to include two aspects of some of the more flexible all-year school designs: (1) the Forty-Five—Fifteen may be rescheduled to permit all students to attend school for four forty-five-day terms with each forty-five-day term followed by a fifteen-day intersession term on an optional attendance basis; and (2) the Forty-Five—Fifteen extended school year design may also be reorganized to permit all students in a community to attend school for four forty-five-day terms with each term followed by a fifteen-day vacation period for all students.

The Nine-Three provides the opportunity for three-fourths of the student population in a school corporation to enroll in school on the first day of the school year. Three weeks later the fourth group of students enters school, and one of the original groups to enter school takes a three-week vacation. After six weeks of school operation, a second group of the original three groups to enter school takes a vacation; and the first group to take a vacation returns to school. After nine weeks of school, the third group of students from the original groups to enter school takes a three-week vacation, thus the Nine-Three rotating cycle is established.

The rotating-term or cycle Forty-Five—Fifteen design also requires the division of the total school population into four "equal" groups but permits only one of the four groups to enroll in school in sequential fifteen-day intervals in order to establish the rotating cycle. Upon the enrollment of the fourth group of students, the first group to enroll takes a fifteen-day vacation. When the first group of students to enroll in school returns from vacation, the second group to enroll takes a fifteen-day vacation; and when the second group of students returns from vacation, the third group to enroll in school takes a fifteen-day vacation. At this point, the rotating cycle of the Forty-Five—Fifteen is established.

In the initial implementation stages of the Nine-Three design, the first group of students designated by school officials to take a vacation will have the first nine-week school term interrupted by vacation after a period of three weeks. The second group of students designated to take vacations from school will have the first nine-week school term interrupted after a six-week school attendance period. The rotating or cycle Forty-Five—Fifteen design eliminates the interruptions in the educational process, but it creates the initial problem of cost in heating, cooling, cleaning, operating, and maintaining school transportation systems and the school plant for one-fourth of the student population during the first three weeks of school and for one-half the student population during the second three weeks of school.

After nine weeks, the Nine-Three and the rotating Forty-Five —Fifteen become identical school operations. Thereafter, all student groups will attend school uninterruptedly for nine weeks or forty-five days and will vacation for three weeks or fifteen days on a rotating basis.

THE EXTENDED SCHOOL YEAR
AND THE ECONOMY

Education in America, public and private, has become a multi-billion-dollar industry during the past quarter of a century. With the recent crises caused by the energy shortage and the current seemingly eternal inflationary spiral, counterbalanced with a "depression," the shortage of goods and services (energy producing products), the mounting pressure on all citizens to acquire some type of formal training, retraining, or in-service training, the increased cost of maintaining the current school staff and service personnel, the cost of making needed additions to the current faculty and staff, the need and desire for new, modern, and better school housing and facilities, and the skyrocketing prices in school construction costs can only cause this multibillion-dollar business to continue to demand vast amounts in increased revenue from the public treasury. Any multibillion-dollar governmental semi-monopoly must have a strong effect upon the economy of a nation. The industry employs millions of teachers and staff personnel at a cost of billions of dollars per year; it purchases millions of dollars worth of equipment and supplies from other industries, especially the book industry, which employs millions of people; it spends billions in construction, construction labor costs, and reaches into and touches the lives of every family and every individual in America. Any contemplation of a variation in the total number of operational hours in an industry that influences the life of every individual in the nation to some extent at some point in time must necessarily have extremely vital implications for the nation's economy.

The Effect of Year-Round Education on the
Travel Industry and the Energy Crisis

The lives of luxury that Americans and peoples in many other countries have lived since World War II have brought the world to the brink of environmental disaster, jeopardizing their health and their way of life. The energy crisis which we faced last summer and the economic crisis which we feel today both serve to warn us that the natural resources of the world are scarce and must be used with all deliberate caution. An individual's vacation and the length of his vacation may be earned by working for the same company over a period of years; but whether or not that vacation is spent lying around home or taking an excursion across the country will depend upon the supply of our natural resources.

The way we are likely to spend our vacations over the next decade and indeed the next century is of grave concern to the travel industry because the travel and tourist industries are completely dependent for their very existence upon the fuel sources of energy used by trains, planes, buses, and cars.

Tourists must be transported or must transport themselves to enjoy the luxurious lives to which they are accustomed and to enjoy the many beautiful sights and wonders of the world. A lack of fuel could make tourism and travel so expensive that the exploration of a full and happy life could only be afforded by the affluent. Tourism as a discretionary use of fuel is in a vulnerable position as the first target of belt tightening during an energy or fuel shortage. People earn their leisure time, and opportunities to enjoy such rewards should not be restricted but broadened.

Neither the tourist industry nor tourism is the cause of the energy shortage; waste is. Men have begun to waste the supply of natural resources at a rate faster than nature can produce the resources in the same or larger quantities. However, all is not lost; if each individual will burn one less gallon of fuel each week, there will be an end to the fuel crisis. Each motor vehicle owner can find a way to accomplish this goal.

When the word "energy" is mentioned, the terms electricity, natural gas, and water should be included. The waste of these resources (heat, air conditioning, and water), by leaving appliances on for hours without use, leaving temperatures set unnecessarily high or low in unoccupied rooms or buildings, ignoring leaky faucets, all cause the loss of billions of units of energy each year.

Prudent use of energy requires maximum efficiency in the use of equipment and machinery. Business or corporations which operate at a profit must use their components to the fullest. Each empty bed in a hotel for a night can never regain the opportunity to acquire that lost revenue. One may apply the same principle to travel by air, motor coach, or train. When seats are not filled, revenue is lost forever. This is not a desire to find more seats by the transportation industry but a search for more people to fill the seats already available.

To many people, the tourist industry seems to be at the mercy of the length of the school year. This industry has its peak periods when schools are closed for vacation periods and slumps when schools are back in session. Officials in the tourist business are constantly trying to devise rates and fares to attract travelers during the off-peak seasons when all of the facilities that cater to the traveler are being underutilized. The off-season for the tourist industry not only loses money for the industry, but also wastes energy in the meantime. The transportation industry keeps its schedule; and the hotels, motels, and tourist attractions are open and use high amounts of energy regardless of the number of paying customers. It is not only from a desire to make a profit but from a desire to conserve energy that we must spread the imbalance of the tourist and travel industries over the entire year without regard for seasons of the year.

Some people maintain that the tourist industry and the travel industry have a booming business during the summer because schools are closed. It has been the contention of some that the situation causes overcrowding of highways, transportation facilities, accommodations, and attractions. An individual and his family may find his well-earned vacation from work spent fighting crowded tourist areas during the three available school vacation months.

The people in the travel industry dread the peak seasons of the year as much as the off-peak seasons. Hotels and motels that had fifty empty beds a few months earlier find that they could use an additional fifty beds that are not available. The same principle applies to seats on the various modes of transportation. A deterioration in the quality of service in tourist entertainment spots and huge amounts of energy consumed result from the need to push equipment beyond the normal capacity during peak tourist seasons of the year. This causes as much waste of energy as the off-peak season. Inordinate demands on mechanical equipment lessen the life and the dollar investment in many necessary and expensive products, and the quality of service and the enjoyment of the traveler decrease considerably.

When the cause of the peak/off-peak season situation is traced, it is found that the chief instigator is the school schedule. Extending the length of the school year or year-round education alone, especially the rotating-term or cycle design or the more flexible design, would level out substantially this undesirable tendency in tourism and travel. Year-round schools would not help during Christmas and Easter, but they would have a tremendous impact upon the travel and tourist industry during the summer months.

Although summer weather is a factor in vacation planning, many areas enjoy finer weather in other seasons of the year. The cherry blossoms, mild weather in spring, and less humid weather in the fall would provide incentive for travelers and tourists to visit Washington, D.C. in seasons other than summer.

It seldom happens in business that one factor alone could do so much to alleviate a crucial problem as the extended school year or year-round education could do to alleviate stresses on the travel and tourist industry. Quality of service to the traveler and profits to the industry would increase, while the energy requirement would decrease if people traveled twelve months per year rather than three.

Year-round or extended school year education is becoming a necessity. As the need to preserve our natural resources increases daily, so will year-round education increase in recognition as an obvious solution to the conservation problem. We can no longer afford to let millions of dollars in school structures lie unused or underused for one-fourth of the year.

Although tourism has had a small effect upon disturbing the ecological balance of nature, the state legislatures in Oregon and Colorado have introduced legislation to control tourist promotion. There is the fear that the summer influx of tourists will disturb ecology. The answer to the problem is not in control of tourist promotion but in leveling off the influx throughout the calendar year. Year-round education would help to do this, and it should be considered as an alternative to banning tourists. State officials who react to tourism in the state by leveling the numbers out over twelve months rather than three are acting in a positive and constructive manner.

Tourism is within the top three revenue sources in 75 percent of our cities and states. It is a necessary revenue producer. Officials in New York City have found that in 1972 the visitors to New York spent an amount of money second only to the garment/fashion industry. It is quite unlikely that any state legislators would want to curtail a revenue producer that falls within the top three of its sources of money.

More tourists will decide to discover America in the future, since the prices of transportation, hotel lodging, and meals in Europe are increasing at an annual rate of 10 to 15 percent. Mere economics will make the exploration of this country more inviting to American tourists.

The four-day work week will be here within the next decade, and with it will come increased emphasis upon leisure time. Tourism is expected to grow as a choice of leisure time activity. If the family leisure time is forced into 25 percent of the year, the quality of the services available at the various tourist attractions and the environment at such attractions will suffer as the number of tourists increases beyond the capacity of our tourist areas to accommodate.

Year-round education holds the key to solutions of a variety of problems, the consumption of our natural resources included. Is it coincidental that the energy crisis posed its greatest threat during the three months of the summer when schools were closed? People use more fuel during the three months of the summer due to a myriad of reasons which stem directly from the fact that their children are out of school.

If year-round or extended school year educational programs were in operation in 99 percent of the schools instead of 1 percent, there would be no threat on our energy levels during the summer. As we encourage the conservation of energy, let us promote the year-round system of education concept. Let us forget the concern for a balance between ecology and tourism and level our tourist activities over twelve months, instead of facing a three-month peak season. Let us equalize our manufactured and natural resources over all four seasons.

Year-round or extended school year education is more than an alternative; it is, and will become ever more, a necessity. Waste not, want not![1]

As many Americans are beginning to discover, there is nothing sacrosanct about "fun in the sun" vacations during the three hot months of the summer season. Americans are also discovering that "fun in the sun" can be acquired at some locations in this country and at various locations around the world year around. The phrase "fun in the sun" does not necessarily serve as a synonym for "summer." A cozy little cottage in a tourist resort near the snow-covered ski mountains and valleys of the West and Northwest may be more inviting for many vacationing families than the blistering sun of summer. Many entrepreneurs and investors in the tourist industry are hastily developing a clientele for winter, spring, and fall tourist attractions.

For years, many companies within the moving, travel, tourist, and resort industries, as well as other job industries, and the clients served by these industries have endorsed the calendar school year. These businesses and industries have endorsed the lengthened school year for the obvious reasons that they are greatly affected by the nine-month school system. Many companies within the moving industry, as well as customers who have moved during the summer months, appreciate what those three months mean in terms of peak summer demands, which at times are virtually impossible to meet. Almost 50 percent of the total number of moves in a year occur in the 17 weeks while schools are closed during the summer. It is obvious that if the moving industry or the other industries in question did not have this peak demand in the summer months, far less investment in manpower and equipment, as well as buildings, would be required, resulting in significantly lower costs, which in turn could be passed on to the customers in terms of less expensive and better quality service. This is a prime objective of many companies and, indeed, of the whole tourist and moving industry. While it may be difficult to establish a significant correlation between the peak demands of the moving industry and the length of the school year, it is much easier to establish a relationship between family vacation periods, the peak demands upon the travel, tourist, resort, and related seasonal job industries, and the conventional length of the school year. Peak summer demands upon the travel industry could be attributed to an individual's desire for the generally acceptable climate of the summer season for moving purposes rather than to any particular type school calendar. People who can afford the luxury of a choice of season in which to move usually prefer the summer, but those who cannot afford such luxury move when they must.[2]

The Length of the School Year and
the Conservation of Energy

Officials of the National Council on Year-Round Education have reported that no operational extended school year program has been adversely affected by the energy crisis, as of this date. The NCYRE has received a number of letters requesting information on year-round operation, in that the writers see year-round schools as a means of saving energy. The response to energy savings that can occur is related to the number of buildings being operated; e.g., if a school operates one school building with air conditioning for 12 months, it seems (no study available to back this hypothesis) that the operational cost would be cheaper than operating two school buildings, with or without air conditioning, for nine months.

Mr. Paul D. Rice, Director of the NCYRE, is in constant communication with administrators and custodians who conduct traditional school programs; they point out that at least part, if not all, of the air conditioning units are operated during the summer for summer office staff, summer school, and the like. The remarks would lead one to believe that schools operating on a traditional calendar do not, *as is often contended*, shut off air conditioning during the summer months, *as is usually assumed to be the case*.

One extensive study on the energy savings has been conducted in Colorado. Colorado has schools operating year-round, as well as on a variety of other time schedules, and school officials in Colorado are conducting research to determine the effects of length of school day and year upon energy consumption.[3]

Comparative Data on Fuel Conservation in a Typical Colorado School

Significant information has resulted from a computer study requested by Dr. Calvin M. Frazier, Commissioner of Education, State of Colorado. This study was designed to predict effects on heat consumption due to various changes in school building operating schedules.

The Will Rogers Elementary School in Colorado Springs was selected as a "typical" Colorado school building. This one-story school has a total floor area of 39,756 feet; has an enrollment of 497 students; was built in the late 1950's, with an addition in the mid-1960's; and has a hot water heating system using unit ventilators in each classroom. About half of the area is internal in nature (four classrooms, a learning center, a multipurpose gym, and some smaller rooms).

The following summary of information was compiled under the direction of Gene B. Martin, P.E., of the Energy Management Consultants of Colorado Springs: (1) What heating fuel would be saved by closing school in January and extending school through June? The savings is 1.6 percent annually. With a special setback to 50°F, the savings is 3.9 percent annually. With a special setback to 45°F, the savings is 5.8 percent annually. With the heating system shutdown and drained during Christmas vacation and January, the savings is 23.9 percent annually. (2) What heating fuel would be saved using four-day weeks in January and February? The savings is 0.7 percent annually. (Temperature setback beyond 55° and

60°F is *not* recommended for short periods of three days or less.) (3) What fuel would be saved by closing school an additional seven days in January (extending Christmas vacation)? The savings is 0.7 percent annually. With a "special" setback to 50°F, the savings is 3.9 percent annually. With a "special" setback to 45°F, the savings is 5.8 percent annually. (4) What heating fuel would be saved using a four-day week and extending school one hour per day one week in June? The savings is 0.7 percent annually. (5) What fuel would be saved if we delayed school starting time to 10:00 a.m., Daylight Savings Time in lieu of 9:00 a.m., Daylight Savings Time? The savings is 2.4 percent annually. (6) What fuel would be saved if we delayed school starting time to 11:00 a.m., Daylight Savings Time in lieu of 9:00 a.m., Daylight Savings Time? The savings is 5.2 percent annually. (7) How much fuel is actually saved with reduced daytime temperatures, using 75°F as the "base" temperature? A temperature of 70°F saves 17.1 percent annually (3.4 percent per degree reduced). A temperature of 68°F saves 23.4 percent annually (3.3 percent per degree reduced). (8) How much fuel is saved using various night setback temperatures? A setback of 5°F (to 65°F) saves 8.5 percent annually. A setback of 10°F (to 60°F) saves 12.1 percent annually. A setback of 15°F (to 55°F) saves 15.2 percent annually.

The data presented above are based upon 1964 actual Denver weather, which represents the most average year over the last 30 years. The school energy use was simulated by using the E cube Computerized Energy Analysis program, which is a nationally recognized computer program.

The importance of using the right setback schedule needs to be emphasized. For example, the study shows: Alteration of setback schedule from "on" at 5:00 a.m. Mountain Standard Time and "off" at 6:00 p.m. Mountain Standard Time to setback schedule of "on" at 7:00 a.m. Mountain Standard Time and "off" at 3:00 p.m. Mountain Standard Time indicates that actual fuel consumption could be reduced by 13.8 percent annually.

If the school faced north-south instead of east-west, the fuel used would be reduced by 3.0 percent annually and reduces the "theoretical" air conditioning load by 30 tons, or by 21.5 percent.

If State Code outside air requirements for classrooms are reduced from 25 percent minimum to 12.5 percent minimum, the savings in heating fuel will be 3.4 percent annually. However, this assumes outside air is properly controlled and is not introduced into the school except from 9:00 a.m. Mountain Standard Time to 3:00 p.m. Mountain Standard Time. For example, if outside air is used until

6:00 p.m., an additional 8.1 percent heating fuel would be required annually. Under no circumstances (other than emergency) should outside air dampers be "deactivated" or sealed closed.

Colorado Springs weather was also used to check the accuracy of the program. This data indicate an error of only 5.9 percent based on actual utility bills. Reference data runs were also made on Pueblo and Eagle, Colorado, and Cheyenne and Laramie, Wyoming weather data.

The data assume that the school heating plant is on an occupied-unoccupied seven-day time clock schedule using 10° of setback from 70°F space temperature (i.e., night setback), unless noted otherwise. Time clock was set to bring heating system "on" two hours before school starting time (9:00 a.m. Standard Time was the "base" time), with outside air off until school actually started. The time clock went to unoccupied setback with outside air off at 3:00 p.m. Standard Time.

Most standard night thermostats cannot be set below 55°F; therefore, special setback methods must usually be used.

Setback temperatures or time duration of setback should be varied with outside ambient and wind conditions. Either smaller setbacks or shorter time schedules should be used during severe weather conditions. Also, different school buildings and systems require varied "recovery" time.[4]

The following information by Dr. Calvin Anderson concerning comparative fuel consumption and projected energy requirements for air conditioning has been released by the Colorado Department of Education. This data is supplementary to that released earlier this year by Dr. Calvin M. Frazier, Commissioner of Education.

This comparative data is also based on the same school building in Colorado Springs that was used for the original study.

As a matter of interest, simulations were run to predict heating fuel consumption of this same school if it were located in the following cities using Denver weather as a data base. The fuel consumptions for these cities are as follows:

CITY	PERCENT OF ANNUAL FUEL
1. Denver	Base
2. Colorado Springs	+ 5.2%
3. Eagle	+ 33.2%
4. Pueblo	– 8.5%
5. Cheyenne (Wyo.)	+ 15.8%
6. Laramie (Wyo.)	+ 37.9%
7. St. Louis (Mo.)	– 10.1%

Using this same school again for comparative data, if air conditioning were added to this test school (nine months) without improving the building insulation, it would add 16.4 percent to the annual electrical consumption of the building.

If, at the same time, this comparative school building were used for summer school, the electrical consumption would jump by 61.2 percent. Why? The KW demand jumps over three times. The effect of the sun and light on the building, plus children in the classroom, accounts for the fact that there is an extreme air conditioning load. Even in Eagle, Colorado, which is relatively a high, cool climate, this factor is present due to the children in the classroom and the excessive amount of sunlight. In fact, year-round school using this building without any changes in the insulation pattern will cost 61.2 percent more in use of electrical energy.

It is significant and of interest to note that computer runs also indicate that the use of air conditioning in the nine-month test school increases the annual heating fuel used by 1.9 percent. In the year-round school, the increase is 4.6 percent. The reason for this additional heating cost with the use of air conditioning is that in an uncontrolled building the heat generated during the day is an excessive amount and remains throughout the night. In a building controlled by air conditioning, the temperature maintained at 72 or 75 degrees at night does not allow the excessive heat build-up. Therefore, any night chill will activate the heating system in an air conditioned building. The uncontrolled building will have been overheated during the day and thereby will have this residual heat to compensate for the chill factor.

Again, using comparative school data and Denver weather as the data base, the following electric power consumption using air conditioning is predicted for the year-round school. (Remember that the Denver base would indicate that the electrical consumption would increase 61.2 percent.)

CITY	PERCENT OF ANNUAL KWH
1. Denver	Base
2. Colorado Springs	– 5.3%
3. Eagle	–11.8%
4. Pueblo	+ 5.7%
5. Cheyenne (Wyo.)	–5.7%
6. Laramie (Wyo.)	– 11.4%

Note: These figures do not apply to residential buildings.

The amount of energy that can be saved by proper thermal treatment of this test school was not studied; however, based on other studies made by the Energy Management Consultants, Inc., it is estimated that 40 percent or more of the annual heating fuel could be saved by proper insulation. This would mean that smaller heating unit plants could be used. Of course, similar savings could be made with air conditioning and air conditioning equipment. This proper thermal treatment would include such items as adding better wall insulation, changing the glass to thermopane, reducing the glass area, shading the glass to control the outside light, or better insulating the roof.

It is also estimated by one expert that turning on the lights during summer school can increase the temperature as much as 10 percent; however, this factor varies with the amount of ventilation available.[5]

The officials of the New Hampshire State Department of Education have analyzed and disclosed a rather comprehensive study of methods to realign the conventional 180-day school year to conserve energy. None of these alternatives dealt with extending the length of the school year. In a letter to superintendents across the state, Commissioner Newell Paire offered the following suggestions and discussed the advantages and disadvantages of each: (1) a ten-day reduction in the school year; (2) closing school during Christmas, winter, and spring vacations with seventeen make-up days in June and July; (3) an extended Christmas vacation through January and February with make-up days in June and July or with Saturday classes in April and May; (4) changing the summer vacation to December, January, and February; and/ or (5) a four-day school week with the loss of time made up by adding one hour and fifteen minutes to each of the four school days.[6]

School Construction and the
Conservation of Energy

We can and must learn to save energy, or the constant decreasing availability of our energy resources will force us to return to the less sophisticated energy sources of bygone years. The real issue becomes whether we can learn to save energy, conduct schools year-round, and fulfill the needs of the human being at the level to which he has become accustomed. There are ways to accomplish all of the previously mentioned tasks and enjoy the aesthetics of architecture at the same time. Buildings in the future must be constructed in a manner to use the forces of nature—the wind, the sun, the rain, the snow, the earth, the cold, and the heat—as substitutes for a portion of the energy needs and for the physical, emotional, and/or intellectual comfort of the individual.

Our challenge for the future is to conserve energy, yes; but we must at the same time preserve the dignity of man. One of a combination of energy conserving measures may be found in year-round operation of schools. The real question to which we have been addressing ourselves is, can year-round operation of the current school plants and facilities within a community conserve more energy than the construction of new school plants designed to conserve energy and to be conducted on a conventional school year schedule? School buildings today waste energy; but through proper school building design, the wasted energy can be saved. Energy shapes buildings, and buildings shape the way people live, work, and play. Energy can be saved without sacrificing aesthetic and human values. We can use less energy and still have buildings, even better school buildings. Buildings, in general, consume an incredible amount of energy—about one-third of all the energy used in this country.

Approximately 40 percent of the energy used in our buildings is wasted. This amounts to a waste of 65 billion gallons of oil each year. Such waste can be saved if we construct our buildings in the correct way. School buildings, as well as other buildings, can be designed to do their jobs without guzzling energy. The construction of a Cadillac building with a Volkswagen engine can save that 40 percent waste factor.

Thirty years ago we had oil and gas rationing, and we walked and used streetcars to get to work. Our children were comfortable in rooms facing the sun during very cold days with no oil-generated heat at all—only heat produced by solar energy. And in the coldest climate. We have past lessons as well as more flexibility than present-day living standards suggest for saving energy.

The more space there is to heat or cool, the more energy that is needed to accomplish the purpose. This assertion is usually true, except in cases of open concept buildings. To conserve energy and conduct school year-round requires that school construction be based upon principles. Each principle of design has as its foundation an underlying principle: function, economy, and form. By using the following principles to underscore the energy component, the basis for designing school buildings to conserve energy may be formed: (1) orientation (The way in which a building is placed on the site can save energy.); (2) solar heat control (Solar heat flows into a building by radiation, convection, and conduction. The solar heat source can be controlled and can result in a reduction in the amount of energy required to heat and cool a building.); (3) solar light control (Using the natural light of day, when possible, to light a building saves energy.); (4) task recognition (When the lighting, heating, and cooling requirements of a building are adjusted to the specific task to be conducted in a building, energy savings will result.); (5) efficiency (If a job can be conducted in minimum floor space, less energy will be consumed.); (6) regionalism (Energy can be conserved when the climate, terrain, natural growth, and local mores are considered in the plans for constructing a building.); (7) wind (The wind can be controlled to help or hinder physical comfort within a building. Directing and modifying the wind on and within a building can conserve energy.); (8) heat flow (Heat flow that is caused by conduction requires insulation to stop it; heat flow caused by radiation requires a reflective material to stop it; and heat flow caused by convection requires a vacuum or "dead air space" to stop it. In order to cause heat flow, take away insulation, the reflective materials, or dead air space.); (9) conditioned outdoors (If the outdoor space is conditioned by modifying the effects of the sun, the wind, and the rain to reduce the inside area, a substantial energy savings can be accomplished.); (10) controls (When certain sections of a building are not in use, opportunities for energy savings are possible if the energy flow to such sections can be cut off.); (11) centralization or decentralization (A centralized or decentralized heating and cooling system depends upon each situation. Either alternative may be beneficial in a given system or situation.); (12) comfort (People can tolerate various amounts of heat and cool depending upon the region of the country in which they live, their social and economic backgrounds, age, and physical makeup; as a result, comfort standards become irrelevant.); (13) building geometry (The shape of a building can save energy.); (14) climate (Use the climate—put the climate to work.); (15) make the envelope (The outside structure of the building should be lean and clean. The more wall and roof space there is the more energy is consumed.); (16) design on the edge of the comfort zone (People can use more or less clothing to suit individual needs.); and (17) use energy efficiency systems (Cooling, heating, lighting, walls, roof components and penetration, and the relationship of wall openings which let in air, light, and view should all be considered.).

It has become an established fact that the many open concept building plans recently constructed or currently under construction consume less energy than the traditional school building designs. The open concept building consumes less heat, less air conditioning, and less electric lighting. The more open, the better. Partitions block off both light distribution and air flow. The open plan for schools comes close to the Cadillac with the Volkswagen engine.

Consider the site. Put trees to work to shelter buildings from unwanted hot sun and cold blowing wintry winds. If on a hillside, bury part of the building! Ground temperature is fairly constant below the frost line. Buildings should be constructed in a location that will avoid combinations of strong wind and low temperature. Buildings should also be constructed in locations that will avoid light and heat reflections from other buildings and surfaces, and from water or ground. Paramount consideration should be given to wind paths, pressure effects, and how wind behaves over topography or around nearby buildings. Think twice before placing buildings on stilts in cold climates.

Less energy and money are lost in open sheltered space than in heated space. With an umbrella-like roof to provide protection from the sun and rain, many activities can be conducted better outside than inside the school building.

If one wishes to save energy, bury a part of the building. The earth is a good insulator. The earth can be used most advantageously in mountainous areas. Courtyards can save energy. If people do some of their living and working in conditioned outdoor spaces, substantial savings in energy will be possible. A successful courtyard saves energy and provides a more humanistic environment than a heated, completely enclosed room.

If we can employ these concepts to reduce the vast amount of energy needed to heat the schools during the cool seasons and to cool the buildings during the warm seasons, the end product should be a net savings in energy consumption in a given building for a year-round period.[7]

FOOTNOTES AND REFERENCES

1. Toohey, William D. "How Will Year-Round Education Affect the Travel Industry?" *Proceedings of the Fifth National Seminar on Year-Round Education* (Virginia Beach, Virginia, 1973), pp. 171-174.

2. Dettmer, Robert G. "Y.R.S. Truly." *Proceedings of the Fifth National Seminar on Year-Round Education* (Virginia Beach, Virginia, 1973), pp. 181-82.

3. Personal letter from Paul D. Rice, Director of the National Council on Year-Round Education, Virginia Polytechnic Institute and State University (Blacksburg, Virginia, January 28, 1974).

4. Frazier, Calvin M. "Computer Report: School Day, Calendar, and Set-Back," Colorado Department of Education (Colorado Springs, Colorado, January, 1974).

5. Anderson, Calvin. "Fuel Conservation of a Typical Colorado School Comparative Data," Colorado Department of Education (Colorado Springs, Colorado, April 30, 1974).

6. "Fuel Storage and the School Calendar." *Coos County Democrat* (Lancaster, New Hampshire), November 29, 1973.

7. Caudill, William W., Lawyer, Frank D., and Bullock, Thomas A. *A Bucket of Oil: The Humanistic Approach to Building Design for Energy Conservation* (April, 1974), p. 87.

THE EXTENDED SCHOOL YEAR AND
CHANGING EDUCATIONAL SYSTEMS

The reorganized school year, rescheduled school year, all-year school, twelve-month school, year-round school, and extended school year are all titles applied to a design of year-round school operations. The terms refer to a lengthened period of the calendar year during which schools are in session and provide a complete program of curricular offerings to pupils beyond the traditional nine-month, 180-day calendar year. There are many educational innovations through which students could realize maximum benefits if the schools of the district were conducted on the extended school year schedule. The extended school year concept as defined and used throughout this account excluded the school districts in whch school officials had extended the school year by implementing the traditional or conventional summer school concept. In many cases throughout this book, I have used extended school year and year-round school as synonymous terms. However, the term "extended school year" is preferred because it encompasses all types of school year designs which lengthen the traditional school year schedule beyond the conventional 180 days.

Some of the more recently designed extended school year programs or variations of programs most definitely lend themselves to the concepts of open education, open space concepts, individualized or personalized instruction, continuity of teaching and learning, continuity of extracurricular programs (band, choir, dramatics, etc.), work-study programs, distributive education, job rotations, flexible scheduling, social and civic organizations, minicourse offerings, elimination of the concept of failure, elimination of boredom in class, enrichment of the educational process, acceleration of the educational process, remediation of the educational process for reluctant learners, increases in the school's holding power, programs for children of migrant workers, improvement of

the professional status of teachers, new school building constructions, the knowledge explosion, the mobile student population,
greater participation in school programs by more students and
different students, and to the concept of quality in educational
programs, etc.

Before we move into a major discussion in this chapter, let me
explain that I see a vast difference between open concept education and open space concept. While open space concept refers to
the construction of a school building without inner walls or with
few inner walls, open concept education is the outgrowth of a
learning and teaching philosophy or theory. Open space lends
itself to this philosophy or theory, but open concept education
can be accomplished within the two-by-four's (four walls of the
traditional classroom and two covers of a book) of the conventional classroom. Open concept education is an attitude toward
teaching and learning which permits a child, in cooperation with
the instructor, to select and explore his own area of learning. Although open space is advantageous to the open concept in education, negative attitudes of teachers toward the concept can soon
create walls made of shelves and racks and can create a classroom
composed of a traditional atmosphere overnight. The design of
a particular school building structure does not create an open
concept approach to education. An open concept approach can be
found in any type building structure if the teachers and the administrators have an open concept to teaching and learning.

I also recognize a vast difference between individualized instruction and personalized instruction. Traditional instruction required
all students in a class to travel down the same academic highway
at the same rate of academic speed, regardless of the condition
of the vehicle. The concept of tracking permitted students with
similar academic abilities to travel down the same highway at
the same rate of speed. Individualized instruction permits each
student to travel down the same highway at his own rate of speed
which respects, to some extent, the condition of the vehicle. In
other words, each student is given the same instructional packet
but is permitted to advance through the packet as swiftly or as
slowly as his physical and mental capabilities will permit. Personalized instruction and the open concept to education permits
each student, in cooperation with his instructor, to choose the route
he will travel and to travel that route at his own pace, recognizing
his needs, wants, desires, and his mental and physical capabilities.
You see, individualized instruction is to personalized instruction
as buying a suit from your local retail store is to having a suit
made by an expert tailor. Every child in a class may wear the same

size suit and must select the same size suit from his local retail store, but the suit will not fit each student the same because of the contour and stature of each individual's body. Likewise, the contour of the students' minds will not permit them to absorb the same material from the traditional teaching-learning process with the same degree of comfort as another student, irrespective of the students' similar or dissimilar mental attributes. If each student has his suit tailored by an exclusive tailor, there will not be another suit that is like it in the class. There most certainly will not be two suits exactly the same because no two people would have exactly the same body build. Personalized instruction is to tailor-make the student's course of study to fit the mental and physical contour and stature of his needs and desires. From this approach should be developed a product well suited to function in a complex society.

Open Concept Education, Individualized or Personalized Instruction, and the Lengthened School Year

The extended school year or year-round school concept could serve as a shot of adrenaline to innovations such as open concept education and individualized or personalized instruction. If the philosophy behind either of the previously mentioned innovations is to take each child where he is academically and permit him to flourish and grow according to his own mental and physical needs and desires, then the length of the school year must not stand as an obstacle to that process. People are not machines; and the rate of academic acceleration of the human mind cannot be predicted as can the rate of acceleration of a motor vehicle traveling along a highway. Some students learn at extremely rapid rates; other students have difficulty learning at all. The decision as to when the academic faucet will be turned on or shut off should become a personal matter between the student (according to his physical and mental capabilities), his teacher, and his parents. In the conventional school schedule we have, in essence, told students when it is time to learn and when it is time to stop learning. Opportunities for academic growth should be constantly available in an individual's life. This means availability of school around the year, and I am tempted to say around the clock. The open concept in education, individualizing instruction, or personalizing instruction are in diametric opposition to the concept of a conventionally scheduled school year. One cannot truly have open education, individualized instruction, nor personalized instruction if the academic work of a year must be completed in less than half (approximately 180 days) of the 365 days in that year. The concept of the traditional school year automatically establishes grade levels or learning levels, passing and failing of grades, and the completion of a representative amount of academic work within a given period of time. These previously mentioned negative issues can only be abolished through year-round education for all students—the reluctant learner and the academically alert. A student cannot progress academically at his own rate nor have his academic suit tailored if there is not all the necessary time possible made available for such processes to run their course. The opportunities for neither open concept education, individualized instruction, nor personalized instruction can be maximized if the schools of a district are conducted on a conventional or traditional school year schedule. Only year-round education for all students, not a rotating-term or cycle design, can accomplish these goals.

The Length of the School Year and Continuity in the Educational Program

It is a reasonably established fact that the acquisition of academic knowledge taught in the schools comes to an abrupt halt when school ends in late spring or early summer and the acquisition starts again when school opens in late summer or early fall. There are even some data available which suggest that most students forget the information taught and learned in school while enjoying the long summer vacations. As a former teacher of English, drama, and music, I can agree with these assertions based upon my own public school experience. Ask any teacher of band, choral music, or dramatics about the amount of time needed in the fall to bring the previous year's performing groups up to the standards to which they had advanced at the close of school the previous year. Ask any one of the same teachers about the amount of forgetting that takes place during the long summer vacation from school; or, better still, listen to and watch these groups perform at the close of school and at the opening of school and compare the two performances for yourself. After one such observation, it is certain that you will agree that students do forget vast amounts of information during the long summer vacation and that several months are needed for re-teaching materials already taught during the previous year. The conventional school year and most rotating cycle designs actually require tooling-up and tooling-down time for all students and teachers, which leaves approximately six months of teaching time each year. Only the selection and implementation of year-round education designs which permit year-round school attendance for all students can eliminate the dilemma and provide a full year of educational opportunities for students of a school corporation.

Year-Round Education and Student Job Opportunities

Extending the length of the school year can have a great effect upon the employment opportunities of students and working mothers. These opportunities may present themselves through school-directed work-study programs, distributive or cooperative education programs, job rotation programs, or flexible scheduling, and through the release of mothers from home industries for the job market. Work-study programs and distributive education or cooperative education programs are all concepts of attending school part-time and working part-time. The work-study program is a program aimed at providing a small amount of money through work for economically deprived students through a matching grant provided by the federal government and the school. The distributive or cooperative education is on-the-job training for a student who has chosen the type of work he wishes to perform throughout life. In this case, the program is directed by school personnel, but the employer pays the student's salary. In both cases, the student attends school part-time and works part-time. The work-study program, the distributive education program, and the cooperative education program all lend themselves to a system of year-round education. Through year-round education, the student could work and complete a conventional year of academic school work in twelve months and graduate from high school on time.

Rotating-term or cycle designs can release the mother from home industries and permit her to actively seek employment by rotating the school vacation periods of older children in the family in a manner that would permit one student to be at home with younger children each school term. This year-round benefit should reduce the welfare roles and/or aid to dependent children substantially. The rotating-term or cycle designs can also eliminate the need for all work-age students to seek jobs during the summer vacation from school. In a rotating-term or cycle design a job may be held during one school term by one student member of a family and held during another school term by another vacationing member of the family, thereby increasing the economic status of the family. The same process can be applied to nonfamily members, thereby eliminating the need for all students of work age to seek employment during the summer months. The positions can be rotated throughout the year; and all students of work age can find employment, rather than only a few students during the summer vacation. Such a process can be of great benefit to economically deprived or poor families.

All of the previously mentioned issues surrounding the year-round approach to education are only made possible because of the enormous amount of flexibility that can be built into the scheduling of students into the year-round programs. The traditional school year will not permit all students who need or desire employment during the summer months to find job opportunities. Many students will be left without jobs as a result of the traditional school year concept; many students, including college students who are in competition with high school students for jobs, are unable to find jobs when all are seeking jobs during the summer vacation from school. We have failed to mention that when schools are conducted on a conventional school year schedule many teachers (expecially male teachers and heads of households) are also in competition with students for the summer vacation jobs.

Schools conducted on a conventional school year schedule permit teachers, who compete with students for summer jobs, to provide an employer with part-time labor of good quality rather than full-time labor on a rotating basis. If these teachers are employed for the summer, it makes the unemployment figures appear worse than they really are, because two jobs have been given to one individual. This does not permit the less qualified workers of our country an opportunity to become self-reliant. Examples of this can readily be found in the travel, tourist, resort, and hotel industries during the summer. We must realize that opposition to an extended school year concept may come from owners of small family businesses that experience great increases in production during the summer months. These increases create a need for older students in the family to help with home and business industries during these peak seasons of the year.

The Extended School Year and Competing Factions

One basic reason that the extended school year concept or year-round education has not gained greater acceptance across this country is the demand for the students' time during the summer months by different civic and social organizations in a community. These demands create a solidified effort on the part of the community which opposes the operation of schools beyond the conventional school year length. Boy Scouts, Girl Scouts, summer camps, college clinics of various types (band, choral, basketball, football, cheerleaders, dramatics workshops, etc.), family vacations, summer employment, 4-H Club, YMCA, YWCA, Boys Club, swimming pools, city parks and recreation areas, Lions Club, Rotary Club, Civitan Club, various church-sponsored organizations, and many other social and civic groups compete with any extended school year arrangement for all or a portion of the time of students during the summer for involvement in a different type educational program. With all these groups demanding the students' time during the summer and the same groups exercising local control over the schools, it becomes extremely difficult for educators to establish a majority consensus needed for extending the length of the school year. Most of these groups feel that they can only operate their programs for students successfully during the three summer months, whereas the school has the remaining nine months of the calendar year for operation; and a majority of these groups feel that the programs provided by their organizations are of equal educational importance to the student as the educational program conducted by the school. Some officials of these organizations feel that their summer education programs are more beneficial to the physical and mental well-being of the students and teachers in light of nine months of rigorous mental or academic exercise. There are arguments that teachers and students need a rest from the academic routines and that the most suitable time of year for other organizations to fill the gap is during the summer months when the weather is more suitable to outdoor life.

Family vacations and the lengthened school year do not come into as much conflict as has traditionally been true because the family vacation periods are now observed throughout the calendar year, not just the summer. Today students and their parents take vacation periods during all seasons of the year. After all, "fun in the sun" can be found year-round someplace in the world, or a family may prefer the snow-capped mountains of Colorado.

The Extended School Year and the Open Space Concept

The new trend in constructing open space buildings is a plus for the year-round operation of schools. Open space buildings use less energy than the egg crates of yesteryear. Less energy is required to light, heat, or air condition open buildings than the conventional or traditional buildings. The truth of this assertion is apparent because there are fewer walls to contain the light, heat, or air. These energies are permitted to flow and glow to maximum potential.

The Extended School Year: An Increase in the School's Holding Power

The implementation of an extended school year program can aid the school in keeping students enrolled or in keeping students from dropping out of school. Some of the techniques provided include offering minicourses, the elimination of the concept of failing, the elimination of boredom in the classroom, enrichment of the educational process, acceleration of the student's academic progress, remediation of the educational process of reluctant learners, greater participation in school programs by more students and different students, and building quality into the school's educational program.

There seems to be something repulsive to the human being about the requirement to remain in any particular course over a long period of time. This is especially true with potential school dropouts and failures. These young people become bored when a long period of time is required to make up any courses failed. This adds "insult to injury" because the opportunities for boredom, the duration of the class, and the possibility of failure are repeated. In many extended school year designs, students are given the opportunity to take minicourses which are taught and completed over a short span of time, can be repeated in a short span of time, and can be completed before the student has time to become bored.

In all extended school year or year-round school designs which require school attendance by all students in the district for an additional number of days during the calendar year and in a few extended school year designs which do not require but may permit extended school year attendance by some or most of the students, opportunities for enrichment, acceleration, remediation, and greater participation by students are presented. Students may use any days added to the school year to accelerate the academic process; to do remedial work in areas of least competency; to take courses which enrich the educational process (those courses that the student wishes to take that are not required for graduation); and to take advantage of the opportunity to participate in band, choir, dramatics, etc.

Teachers have complained that a decrease in the quality of their programs has resulted from a lack of available time in which to build quality into the programs. Some designs of the lengthened school year (especially the flexible designs) will provide as much or as little time as needed to ensure quality programs for students. Additional time is also provided to cope with the knowledge explosion. Each year there comes into existence an insurmountable amount of new knowledge to be absorbed by the human mind. The mind is now capable of absorbing only a fraction of the new knowledge as well as a fraction of the historical data already available. Extended school year designs which require or permit extended school year attendance by students can provide a forum upon which inroads can be made into the acquisition and retention of greater amounts of knowledge.

The Extended School Year and Professional Negotiations

It is quite likely that the extended school year or year-round concept could aid in the elimination of professional negotiations and return a degree of the lost "professionalism" to the teaching ranks. It is my personal conviction that teachers as a whole across the country are satisfied with their monthly pay checks when those checks are paid in installments equal to the number of months the teachers actually work. Teachers become dissatisfied when their nine- or ten-month checks must be spread over a twelve-month school year in order to make ends meet, when other sources of employment must be sought during the three months of summer, and when needed employment is not found during the summer months. It is at this point that teachers become angry and attempt to secure enough money from the school officials for nine or ten months work to support them over a twelve-month period. It is quite frustrating to work half the next year to repay bills left unpaid during the previous summer and continue to meet additional obligations as they come due. Give the teachers twelve months employment at twelve months pay and destroy the negotiations table, tactics, and hostilities. Although money is not the only item sought when negotiating, it is usually the item of paramount concern.

Year-Round Schools and the Migrant Worker

The migrant worker, whether a United States citizen, a South American citizen, or a citizen of Mexico, usually travels from one place to another or from one region to another with his family, including school-age children, in keeping with the crop harvest. As a result, many of the children of these families have been permitted or forced to forego their academic or cognitive development due to lack of schooling. A rotating-term or cycle design or a more flexible extended school year design could aid in alleviating this unfortunate situation. The rotating-term or cycle designs would permit students to enter school and complete courses in twenty days, forty-five days, four months, sixty days, or three months, depending upon the type of extended school year design implemented. Some of the more flexible extended school year designs would permit students to enroll and withdraw from school at any time necessary. Although this arrangement would provide neither the best quality of schooling nor the smoothest transitions for the students, the opportunity for some schooling throughout the calendar year is better than no schooling at all. The previously explained advantages of extending the school year would apply not only to students of migrant workers, but also to students of any family that finds it necessary to move at inconvenient times during the year in this extremely mobile society of ours. Schooling would also bring certain social services as a by-product to each of these students. Students could receive at least two hot, well-balanced meals per day, free medical and dental care, free clothing, and some work-study opportunities; and smaller children may be exposed to day-care facilities. Such school arangements would also make it possible for students entering school for the first time to enter school in closer proximity to the age restrictions as prescribed by state law. Such restrictions have caused some students to lose a year in school by entering school a year late.

Improving the Professional Status of Teachers

It comes as no surprise that teachers actually work less than half the year if one subtracts approximately 180 days from 365 days in the year. However, 104 of the remaining days are Saturdays and Sundays. Looking at it from this standpoint, most people who propose to work all year only work eighty-one days more per year than teachers, unless they are employed for six or seven days per week. Some also wish to discuss that teachers work a shorter day than most other employees; but, in such conversations people always seem to forget that most competent and energetic teachers work long hours at night in an effort to complete work from the previous day or days or to plan meaningful experiences for the students in the future. In spite of these ventures and the fact that the teacher is obligated to the school district for nine or ten months, he is put into a position of subsisting for nine months at an economic level below that of the recent graduates from his school who are employed at the local factory, or he relegates his standard of living to that of the poverty-stricken by having his nine-month salary paid in twelve or twenty-four installments. He receives twelve installments if he is paid by the month and twenty-four if paid on a biweekly basis. We will not discuss the salaries of the doctors, lawyers, engineers, politicians, and judges who are successful because of or in spite of our teaching efforts. The previous discourse has been inserted as a prelude to the assertion that the professional and economic status of teachers should be improved. Teachers need to draw year-round salaries for around-the-year employment. They should not be forced to join the unemployed and accept positions of common labor alongside their students, graduates, patrons, and parents. This is a constant blow to the teaching profession and a source of comfort and laughter to the less academically qualified. Many well-qualified teachers have been forced to abandon the teaching profession because of the nine-month work-pay arrangement. For many of these teachers, abandonment of the profession is with deep regret because they love teaching. But how can one continue to teach and watch his family live in poverty for at least three months of the calendar year?

The Extended School Year and Performance or Competency-Based Criteria

As we explore the concept of competency-based criteria, I always become preoccupied with the question of whose competency is under consideration. Are we concerned with the competency of the instructor, or are we concerned with the performance or competency of the students after they have been exposed to the expertise of the instructor? Once this question has been answered, then we may be about the business of assessing the effects of the extended school year concept upon the criteria. It seems to me that we are concerned about the competency of the students' performance in a subject matter area after a particular course has been completed. If a majority of the students can perform well in an area after having been exposed to the quality instructions of a teacher, then the teacher is competent. If a majority of the students cannot perform well after having been exposed to a teacher, then the teacher is incompetent. The competency of the student is of utmost concern; the competency of the teacher is a fortunate or unfortunate by-product of the teaching-learning process. In either case, the extended school year concept which eliminates the long vacation period in which a student forgets a vast amount of cognitive knowledge (the lack of continuity in learning) can increase the perceived competency of the performance of a student or the teacher. The long periods necessary for re-teaching after a long vacation, the periods of cranking-up and winding-down, must also improve the perceived competency or performance level of both parties involved. In a rotating-term or cycle design, shorter periods for evaluation of performance and competency are available; this permits a student to be evaluated before he forgets pertinent information.

The Extended School Year and School Desegregation

It has been my contention even since I was a teenager that the desegregation of schools was not the best route to equality in the American society. Yet, I understand the attack upon schools as the most likely vehicle through which desegregation could be accomplished. School was the most fluid of all our American institutions. They belong to all the people because all the people paid for them. Blacks have paid more than their fair share based upon the economic rewards for their labor and the quality and quantity of property owned by most. In all too many cases, the small portion of funding allocated to black schools was diverted to use in white schools. It is my contention that the long-range problems to be solved are quality of education and equity of success in adult life, but the short-range problem is housing and economics for blacks and poor whites. Housing, of course, is directly tied to economics. I come to this conclusion when I watch poor black and white bodies tortured from a day's work for which they receive only sub-minimum wages.

Through the years, members of poor families have come together and pooled their efforts during vacation from school in order to purchase adequate clothing for the next year of school. All members of the family who were old enough to find odd jobs of any type were called upon to contribute their share.

A rotating-term or cycle extended school year design could prove beneficial to poor families if the family contained enough members of work age to rotate a job year-round. This would bring an additional salary into the home and could thereby raise the family's standard of living. Extended school year designs which require extended school year attendance by all students of the district would eliminate the opportunity to add the additional salary to the family income and to provide suitable school clothing for the student members of the family. Such designs or the lack of finance could even cause students of legal age to discontinue their schooling. After all, what head of household would want to expose his children to economic affluence without the opportunity to at least appear affluent or, at the very least, not to appear poverty-stricken? Money can purchase housing in an integrated neighborhood, and money can provide economic affluence. A day's pay for a day's work to each individual is the starting point toward the successful integration of a society, but some extended school year designs will not permit a day's work for any school-age children.

The Extended School Year and Administrative Decentralization

The decentralization of local school corporations, districts, or systems in various cities across this country has been implemented in two basic designs and in variations of each of those designs. The two designs are administrative decentralization and political decentralization. Administrative decentralization is the process of dividing a large school district into several geographical areas and delegating administrative authority for each area to an area superintendent who reports to the superintendent in charge of the entire school corporation. Political decentralization is the result of the power of the community pressure groups to usurp by force the authority for the administrative control and operation of the schools within a geographical region of a school corporation from a legally constituted centralized authority. Each geographical area of a school corporation in which political decentralization has become a reality may have a mini-school board. Either type of decentralization may have community advisory boards to various administrative units in each area, depending upon the needs and desires of the community. There is some concern about the mini-school board concept and the legality of the authority of the local district school board to delegate its power to another board or commission.

If an extended school year or year-round school program is to be implemented as a pilot or experimental project, having the district divided into areas and designating one area as the experimental area may have some advantages. However, people in other areas of the community could become concerned over the source of financing the project and could feel that the project should have been financed in their area. If the type of decentralization implemented in a community is political and since most large cities still consist of large elements of de facto segregation, attempts to have complete community areas attend school at the same time and vacation at the same time may become impossible.

The preference is to have members of the same family and the same neighborhood attend school at the same time in order not to destroy community living patterns, but the implementation of such designs in some cities may result in school segregation by school terms.

The Extended School Year and the Financing of Public Education

The process of financing public education by property taxes has come under a good deal of fire over the past four or five years. A great deal of the fire has been generated because the property taxing system can no longer generate, without strong public opposition, the necessary sums of money to continue to conduct a first-rate school system. The property tax has also been criticized because of the vertical (inability to treat economic unequals as unequals) and horizontal (inability to treat economic equals as equals—regressive) inequities, inadequacy of the yield, effect upon market decisions, ability to be shifted or hidden where renters are involved, inconvenience of distance to travel in some cases, and the cumulative amounts to be paid.

Several court cases in recent years have been aimed at dismantling the use of the property tax as a basis for distribution or redistribution of funds for public education.

With these issues as a backdrop to the current state of the economy, the taxpayers will be reluctant to finance any innovative program that will increase the cost of school operations. Year-round or extended school year programs which require or encourage extended school year attendance by all students of a school corporation are known to increase the operational costs of the school. It is quite improbable that a rotating-term or cycle design can save the district taxpayers money. A rotating-term or cycle design cannot be conducted year-round at a cheaper price than a conventional school year program in the same school. The rotating-term or cycle design can be conducted at a savings only when new school construction, facilities, supplies, and renovations are required to continue school operations on a traditional school year schedule.

The Extended School Year and Compulsory School Attendance

Beginning with Massachusetts in 1852 and extending to Mississippi in 1918, each of the forty-eight states had enacted compulsory education laws. The new states of Alaska and Hawaii also have such provisions. The question of minimum school attendance for the child was no longer a decision for the parents but for the state. Some southern states, as a part of their resistance to school desegregation, have enacted laws requiring the closing of public schools before the mixing of black and white pupils is to be accepted. This, in effect, may repeal the compulsory attendance laws in those states. Again, however, it should be noted that this is a governmental and not an individual decision.[1] To many advocates of "States Rights," the Tenth Amendment to the Bill of Rights serves as documented proof of the founding fathers' desire to have education matters controlled by each respective state without federal intervention. Those who favor minimal federal intervention into "state" educational matters have found implied documentation in the Constitution and the Bill of Rights through which the federal government could function in state educational matters through grants of money, grants of land, and court decisions. Of course, the Sixth Amendment of the Bill of Rights gives the federal government the right to lay and collect taxes and excises. Today, advocates of a more liberal education agree that compulsory attendance is illegal because the First Amendment grants freedom of assembly, not forced assembly. Whatever your position on this issue, the extended school year or year-round concept will have some direct or indirect effect upon this law. In states where the compulsory school attendance law is based upon a student's age and rotating-term or cycle extended school year designs permit some students to accelerate the academic process or where extended school year designs are implemented which require and/or encourage students to accelerate the academic process, the school attendance laws will need to be rewritten. Acceleration of the academic process could permit a student to complete high school before he reaches the legal age to discontinue his school attendance. In states where it is possible to accelerate the academic process by two or three years, the law would need to include age and academic attainment clauses which could call for some post-high school training in cases where students graduated from high school at an early age.

Many students quit school because of boredom, impersonalization of instruction, individual academic failure, and a lack of opportunities for remedial work. In a rotating-term or cycle design, the school terms are usually short enough to eliminate boredom, and any courses failed or remedial opportunities desired can be provided in a short school term permitting a student to remediate his academic process or repeat a course failed in a short term and continue to be promoted with his peers. In nonrotating or cycle designs, the personalized approach to teaching may make a student feel comfortable with school and his own progress in school.

The Extended School Year and Ability Grouping

The concepts of ability grouping and year-round education or year-round school attendance are incompatible concepts. Year-round education for all is based upon a philosophy of personalized instruction. If the instructional process is truly personalized, there will be no groups because no two people are alike. Each student will progress academically according to his own capabilities, needs, wants, interests, and desires. There will be no attempt to place those students who seem to be progressing at the same academic rate into groups. The grouping process has basically served to make classroom work easier for teachers and to discriminate against or for students on the basis of their observed mental capabilities. These observations may be made through a number of educationally sanctioned techniques.

The Extended School Year and the Separation of Church and State

Although state-supported schools are in financial trouble, the issue becomes more apparent as we turn our attention to the well-established church-related schools. Outstanding, well-established church-related schools are constantly being closed all across the country due to a lack of necessary funding. In certain areas of the country, these schools represent approximately 50 percent of the schools in the state. If these institutions are forced to close now, all the additional expenses incurred in the transition and maintenance of an extended school year program can only hasten additional closings unless a court interpretation of a constitutional provision grants the use of public funds to finance education in parochial schools. The implementation and competition of an extended school year or year-round school concept can only hasten the death of many fine church-related schools and bring an enormous influx of students into the public sector. Compulsory extended school year legislation without provision for public aid to private, church-related schools would make it impossible for such schools to continue to function. The fly-by-night, segregationist academies are not included in this group of well-established, church-related schools.

The Extended School Year and
Performance Contracting

Performance contracting, the process of contracting with private industry or, in some cases, with individual teachers of a school corporation to raise a student's academic skills in a particular area to a predetermined level within a predetermined time span, has enjoyed its "academic honeymoon" in most school corporations, and the corporations have sought and received a legal separation, if not a divorce. The divorce may never come because the impact of change has been left at the altar in each community when the vows of innovation were solemnly and mutually made. In other words, those communities that accepted performance contracting accepted the challenge to change and innovate, and once the life's blood of change and innovation flows freely through the veins of a community, the community will never be stagnant again. The community will continue to change or will revert to ultra-conservatism.

The basic advantage for performance contracting to be found in the process of lengthening the school year appears to be the element of time. A contract may be written for the duration of all available days in the calendar year or for a period as short as fifteen, twenty, or forty-five days. If the contract is written in only two academic areas (reading and mathematics, for example), the contract could be written for six hours per day, three hours per class. Such a fifteen-day arrangement would equal a traditional nine-week school term. Most experts seem to agree that contracts written for short periods of time enhance the possibility of the contractors increasing their earnings per child. A rotating-term or cycle design would permit a company to receive a handsome reward before the "halo effect" of the motivation techniques used by the company to increase its profits on each student would have an opportunity to wear off. It seems quite likely that the most desirable plan for the contractor would be the forty-five—fifteen designs in which all students of a school corporation attend school for four forty-five-day terms throughout the calendar year interspersed with fifteen-day intersession courses. The fifteen-day intersession periods may prove most beneficial to the contractors. The four-one-four-one-one concept may offer the performance contractors advantages equal to those of the forty-five—fifteen. The longer the duration of the contracts, the greater the financial savings to a school corporation seems to be the general consensus of educators who are experienced in the field of performance contracting. In that case, a year-round contract or a contract that continues around several years may be in the best interest of the taxpayers. The "halo effect" and the novelty of the innovation, the gimmicks, and the motivational techniques will have normalized as well as any instant gains in academic progress, which cannot pass the test of time. After all, the ability to survive (transcend) the test of time was one of the major criterion by which we separated our best music, sculpture, literature, philosophies, concepts, innovations, and many of our most delicious beverages from the mediocre. However, that day seems to be swiftly approaching its end as the concept of greatness becomes synonymous to overnight success. Today the test of greatness seems to be: How well did it sell? If it sold and made millions of dollars, then the evaluated item was and is great.

The Extended School Year and the Nongraded School

At this point, I suppose it is necessary to differentiate between ungraded and nongraded schools. Nongraded schools as herein described refer to schools without grade levels (first, second, third, fourth, etc.). Ungraded schools refer to those schools in which the use of letter grades (A, B, C, D, F, I, etc.) has been discontinued. The process of implementing an ungraded school and the process of implementing an extended school year or year-round school program seem to have little or no apparent influence upon each other. However, the process of replacing grade levels with learning levels is of utmost importance if the concept of year-round school attendance for all or a portion of the students in a school district is mandated or permitted. The concept of personalizing instruction, which must include opportunities for student acceleration and remediation or enrichment of the academic process, could exist with the concept of grade levels but would be restricted by such tradition. The concept of grade levels requires promotions; and promotions, though not necessarily, imply the acquisition of at least average mastery of a certain amount of knowledge within a certain time span. The concept of completing a given amount of schoolwork within a given time span is consistent with the rotating-term or cycle extended school year concept unless a student is permitted to attend school for a period of time beyond the traditional school year, but the concept of time limitations (grade levels) on the acquisition of a body of knowledge is not consistent with the concept of extending the length of the school year for all students of a school corporation. Three of the basic reasons for extending the school year for all students of a school corporation are to permit acceleration or enrichment of the students' academic process, to permit opportunities for remediation for reluctant learners, and to eliminate the concept of failure in school. If these goals are to be accomplished through the personalization of instruction, there can be no point at which students are promoted. If some students are promoted from one grade to another, then it is logical that other students must fail to be promoted. The educational process in the extended school year for all students of a school corporation must be a product of the continuous learning cycle, not one in which the cycle ends at various stages along the academic route to graduation. Personalization of instruction will provide the continuous learning cycle and the elimination of the concept of grade levels. Students in "first grade" who begin moving through academic materials at a rate consistent with their own capabilities will soon cause a class to lose the identity of a self-contained class because some students enter school at various learning levels along a continuum from kindergarten through "second grade" or the second learning level. As students remain in school, the differences in their mental and social capabilities will become apparent.

The Extended School Year and Student
Accidents, Illnesses, and Truants

Unfortunately accidents, illnesses, and truants continually occur among the student population of any school corporation. Accidents and illnesses also occur among faculty members of any school corporation. These situations cause problems for school people, who have selected a variety of ways to cope with each problem. The variety of ways in which problems of illness and/or accidents are handled include (1) granting permission to do make-up work upon the presentation of a doctor's statement; (2) leaving the necessary punishment and/or grading to each individual teacher of the child; (3) instituting a program of home-bound instruction (A teacher is paid by the school district to teach the child at home until such time as the child is physically able to return to school.); and (4) permitting the student to enroll in correspondence courses while ill or injured. In cases of truants, students are dropped from school for the remainder of the school term after they have missed an excessive number of school days, as determined by the school officials. In some school districts, judges have recognized that the basic responsibility for the truancy of a student rests with the parents of the child, and the parents are involved and even penalized for the continued truancy of their child. Many community school officials have hired truant officers, attendance officers, or attendance teachers to aid the home in dealing with the problem of truants. Other communities have special detention or reform schools for students who insist upon breaking school policies.

All extended school year programs currently in operation in this country can accommodate a high degree of flexibility in the students' attendance patterns. Most rotating-term or cycle designs can permit a student to miss a term from school and still make up the term during the same calendar year without loss of time. The basic problem would occur if the student's absence from school should begin in one term of the school year and extend into another term. However, most of the flexible extended school year designs can permit a student to be absent from school on a variety of schedules as long as the student attends school the minimum number of days required by law in his respective state or school community during a calendar year. The amount of flexibility permitted in the attendance and vacation patterns of students is determined by the particular extended school year design implemented in a school corporation. A review of the various extended school year designs in Essays One and Two of this book would explain in detail the many attendance and vacation options available. Only the Multiple-Trails design and one variation of the Forty-Five—Fifteen design (the two designs in which the traditional school year of approximately 180 days is spread over the entire calendar year) would not permit attendance and vacation flexibility during the school year for students unless the students could time the absences during the predetermined school vacation periods.

The Extended School Year and Curricular Improvements

The development of the school curriculum may be defined as building quality into existing programs or broadening the school program by adding many new courses of enrichment, remediation, and/or academic (college preparatory) classes. While building quality into programs is highly desirable and a motivating force behind the positive expressions toward the implementation of an extended school year program, a count of new course offerings in a program provides the most obvious and measurable evidence of the worth or lack of worth of the extended school year or year-round concept in education.

As I converse with educators all across this country who are currently conducting extended school year or year-round school programs concerning the curricular improvements in the school corporation as a result of implementing the extended school year program, they (the administrators) proudly refer to the number of new courses added to the school curriculum for the academically capable students, for the reluctant learners, and for the educational enrichment of all students. The number of courses added to the curriculum in various schools ranged from a low of 1 to a high of 1,400. In some cases, I begin to wonder if courses have not been added to fill space or simply for the sake of adding courses. As I hear of such course titles as "Choral Music for Those Who Can't Sing," "Piano for Those Who Can't Play," or "Art for the Non-Artistic," the previous thoughts rush down the backroads of my mind; but as a teacher with ten years of experience in directing public school choral music, I suddenly remember how beneficial these courses can become. Students develop an appreciation for the arts, and talented students who can make great contributions to the established performing groups are identified.

The Extended School Year and the Professional Growth of Teachers

In this day of the knowledge explosion, the most difficult task faced by a teacher is keeping abreast of the current trends, issues, and innovations in education as well as in his major discipline. Unless a teacher is employed in an extended school year program in a community which also has a college or university campus, opportunities to attend school for personal and professional growth will be drastically curtailed. Nonrotating extended school year designs are *usually* based upon year-round employment for all teachers of the district. The Continuous Four-Quarter plan in Atlanta, Georgia, is presently an exception to this rule because it is currently being conducted on a limited basis. Such designs leave the employed teachers with only their evenings, nights, and weekends free for additional college or university preparation. The rotating-term or cycle designs could pose the same problems if all teachers were employed for the entire year; however, the rotating of teachers will *usually* permit some opportunities for college and university work, providing the college or university is within reasonable access or is on the same schedule as the rotating-term or cycle design of the school district in question. It should not be felt that this is an impossible situation. More and more college officials are moving college personnel across the states and across the region to the people in isolated locations to teach the classes needed or desired by the local school people. Where the distance is too great, there are a few schools that are beginning to fly the professors to the location. In other cases, the professor is permitted to drive the distance, spend the night, and have the college pick up the expense account. I suppose the most difficult problem posed by extended school year employment is inconvenience of access for the teachers and the college officials.

The Extended School Year and School Divisions

Any school district officials who implement an extended school year acceleration design and then permit students to accelerate the academic process to a maximum of the students' capabilities cannot avoid running into trouble with a few students who are extremely capable academically. Instead of using the acceleration extended school year design to reduce the total school and/or the classroom population, the extent to which a student can accelerate the academic process should be restricted unless the student is already below grade, peer group age, or learning levels. Although a reluctant learner is below his grade level, an acceleration design extended school year program can permit the reluctant learner to complete his academic training earlier than he would have under a traditional school year schedule. Premature acceleration through grade levels, elementary school, middle or junior high school, and/or high school could produce students who are too young to graduate and move to another level or too immature to associate with the students of their academic circle. A graduate from high school may be too young and immature for college work and too immature to enter the job market. Unless all schools of the same school corporation are on the same extended school year schedule, a student could run into long vacation periods before the school term of the next school that he will enter reaches an entry point in the cycle or schedule.

The Sociological and Psychological Effect of the Extended School Year upon Student Promotions and Failures

Ever since the professional teacher found that knowledge could not be forced into the heads of students by requiring that the students accept beatings, sit in the dunce corner, stand on one foot for hours, pick up trash, clean the school premises, nor through constant embarrassment or ridicule, the teacher has relied upon the fear of failing a class and the rewards of promotions to motivate students to perform their class assignments. Any student who performed academically according to the "arbitrary and capricious" standards of acceptability set by the teacher is permitted to pass on to the next grade. Any student who fails to perform according to these standards is retained in the class, permitting a younger group of students who are not likely to be his peers to crystalize the visibility of his failure. Many teachers will retire with the honors and pass from the scene without knowing the damage they have done through these indirect lessons of failure they have taught. We have taught people to fail and to succeed, and we have damaged them sociologically and psychologically for life by reinforcing their successes and failures in school with the little letter grades of reward and punishment. We as teachers have taught the lessons of competition, and in all too many cases we have taught that lesson too well. We have taught people to compete and succeed by winning through whatever method necessary—win! It is this attitude that brought us the atrocities in Viet Nam, the Watergate, the uncertain economy, and the energy crisis. It was not a part of our conscious intent to overteach such lessons, but we did. Yet, I see hopeful signs that lessons in "cooperative competition" are once again being taught. I served as a judge for the Miss Southern Baptist College contest in Walnut Ridge, Arkansas, when twenty young ladies were competing for the title. The young lady who won the contest had played piano to the best of her ability (As a music major in undergraduate school, I feel qualified to make this assertion.) for five or six of her competitors as they performed their talent numbers. To me, this was a lesson in "competitive cooperation."

The extended school year or year-round concept in education can reduce the anxiety of competition in school and can reduce the visibility of failure for students. In a rotating-term or cycle design, a student may use the extra term or terms created within the calendar year to repeat any courses in the same year and in a relatively short time span, and he is then ready to be promoted with his peer group. In the nonrotating flexible designs, the element of competition and passing and failing are greatly reduced by the personalization of the educational process. Grade levels to fail are deemphasized, and students are permitted to move through learning levels at their own pace. Students will become accustomed to watching everyone progress at a different rate or work on different academic materials at different locations in the materials. They will even become accustomed to different people working with totally different materials.

The Extended School Year and Vocational- Technical Education

Vocational-technical education needs to be taught around the year, especially in sections of the country where the seasons of the year are more pronounced than in other sections of the country. Certain outdoor vocational-technical jobs need the warm, clear days of spring, summer, and fall to be successfully performed or taught. Other skills that do not require the blessings of the previously mentioned weather conditions can be taught during the cooler days of the late fall, the winter, and the early spring. Other courses which require skills that are likely to be performed indoors can be taught during seasons of the year when it is not so pleasant outdoors.

Many persons who select vocational or technical training as their avocation may require more time to learn the skill of the profession than students who are more academically oriented. In such cases, year-round school attendance for vocationally oriented students would release the time needed to complete the technical training and enter the productive job market.

The Extended School Year and Professional Training of Students

More and more academically capable students are selecting alternative fields of concentration because of the number of years required to complete the training in their preferred field of chosen work. Young men and women of today feel extremely frustrated and repulsed at the thought of spending the currently required number of years in professional schools to become specialists in internal medicine, brain surgery, cardiology, or constitutional law.

The extended school year or a year-round school design which permits year-round school attendance by all or a portion of the student population and also permits maximum acceleration of the academic process by those students can produce the previously mentioned specialists long before the individuals reach age thirty or thirty-five. Neither the number of classes nor class hours would be reduced, but an additional year of study could be accumulated over every three, four, or five years, depending upon the extended school year design implemented. Students could enter college and complete college requirements at an early age and could enter and complete the professional school of their choice at an earlier age than their predecessors.

The Extended School Year and Merit Pay for Teachers

Merit pay for teachers is directly linked to the performance of the students under the teachers' supervision over a designated period of time. The period of time, usually one year, is agreed upon by the hiring agency (school board) and the teacher. I prefer the concept of merit pay referred to as "performance contracting" in Cherry Creek, Colorado. Under this system, teachers receive their base pay but are paid a mutually predetermined bonus for each child who can perform beyond norm expectation at the end of the designated period. In the regular merit pay systems, the amount of a teacher's raise each year is based upon his worth or lack of worth to the school corporation as determined by the teacher's superordinates and/or colleagues.

If the designated time span for measuring the student's educational growth is one year, then a full year-round program of education for all children of the district could only give the teacher a longer span of time in which to have the children improve their skills in basic subjects. We still recognize that short periods between the measurement of the students' achievement levels are always in the teacher's favor. Usually a teacher does not have the opportunity to measure the students' achievement or have the students' schievement measured in short durations of time. If the teacher should have the opportunity to have a student's educational growth measured in short time spans, some type rotating-term or cycle designs should prove beneficial, and the teacher's pay should be increased accordingly.

Energy Conservation, the Economy, and the Year-Round School

Extended school year programs or year-round school programs also lend themselves to the new concepts in building constructions. This facet of this essay was discussed in depth in the previous essay. The modern concept in school construction deals with the concept of energy conservation. Many new school buildings are constructed in a manner to consume less energy to heat in winter, less energy to cool in summer, and less energy to light the buildings all year round. The total annual cost of energy is usually reduced for a new construction even when the conventional school year is lengthened.

Many industries (especially the moving industry) must construct, heat, light, and/or cool vast storage areas that are only needed during the peak moving season of the year—the summer. Likewise, there is a purchase of excess machinery and equipment as well as an extreme increase in the hiring force. Year-round or extended school year programs could eliminate the unnecessary construction and usage of energy and could spread the job opportunities over the entire calendar year. The same basic principles apply to the travel, hotel and motel, and resort industries of this country. Many of our observations (I am certain) can be applied to many other industries in our industrial society.

The Extended School Year and the Small Family Delicatessen

To the small delicatessen owner who has placed his shop near the school campus, the concept of extended school year operations is a profitable idea. While he has been serving the school population for nine months of the year, he can now enjoy the results of a thriving business for twelve months of the year. This is especially true in cases where students are permitted to leave the school campus during lunch hours and recess. However, some benefits are to be derived by the owner of the business when students are en route to and from school each day.

FOOTNOTES AND REFERENCES

1. Campbell, Ronald R.; Cunningham, Luvern L.; McPhee, Roderick F.; Nystrand, Raphael O. *The Organization and Control of American Schools.* Second Edition. (Columbus, Ohio: Charles E. Merrill Publishing Company, 1970).

SUMMARY

In the introduction of this book and throughout the main text, a number of controversial issues have been raised which were included and considered in our survey of year-round education programs. The purposes of the survey were: (1) to identify schools and/or school districts in which extended school year or year-round school programs were currently in operation in each of the fifty states of the United States of America; (2) to identify schools and/ or school districts in the United States of America where year-round or extended school year programs had been implemented and abandoned since 1956; (3) to identify schools and/or school districts in the United States of America in which year-round or extended school year programs were to be implemented in the near future; (4) to determine the type of extended school year or year-round programs and variations of programs conducted or to be conducted in each school district identified as part of the study population; (5) to determine the extent to which each year-round or extended school year design or variation of a design had or had not permitted district officials to achieve a common set of year-round school objectives found in the literature and presented throughout this book.

The investigation was conducted in two phases. Both phases were conducted by survey questionnaire instruments. The first phase was the identification of the year-round or extended school year study population by state school officials, officials of the National Council for the Study of Year-Round Education, and a review of the literature related to the investigation. The second phase of the study was an investigation into the organization, philosophy, and effects of the year-round concepts in local school districts. Survey instruments were mailed to state and local school officials.

The study population was composed of all schools and/or school districts in the United States of America in which some type of year-round or extended school year program was currently in

114

operation, had been implemented and abandoned since 1956, or was to be implemented in the near future.

Those issues previously mentioned throughout this text that were easily resolved were as follows: (1) identification and location of the various types of extended school year designs; (2) rationale for implementation of extended school year programs in the respective school districts; (3) administrative problems related to each type of design; (4) methods of financing extended school year programs; (5) flexibility of state legislation on the implementation of school year designs; and (6) community acceptance of extended school year designs.

A second set of issues encountered throughout this investigation was much more elusive, and a resolution satisfactory to both the opponents and the advocates of year-round education is not likely to be forthcoming within the next three-quarters of a century. In other words, the same issues that have been the main contentions of the advocates and the opponents of year-round schooling during the past three-quarters of a century will be debated for the next century even though the social, economic, and educational status of our country and the world will have thrust us into year-round school operations on a wide scale long before the turn of the century. Many of the issues upon which educators and lay people alike disagree concerning year-round school operations center around the worth or lack of worth of the concept in the following areas: (1) Does the extended school year or year-round concept in education actually save money? (2) Are curricula improvements possible in extended school year situations? (3) Does the extended school year or year-round school year program decrease student attrition rates and increase the holding power of the school? (4) Does the extended school year or year-round concept permit accleration of alert students and provide opportunities for reluctant learners to maintain or acquire desirable grade level or learning expectations? (5) Does year-round education deter juvenile delinquency? (6) What are the effects of year-round or extended school year attendance upon the mental, physical, and/or social well-being of teachers and students?

The most complex, difficult, and elusive issues to which proponents and opponents of the extended school year concept are seeking resolutions and upon which we spent an enormous amount of blood, brain, sweat, time, and tears are as follows: (1) Which extended school year or year-round school program is likely to save the largest amount of money? (2) Which plan permits the greatest number of curriculum improvements? (3) Which plan is most acceptable to the taxpaying public as perceived by school officials? (4) Which design has the most positive effect upon decreasing student attrition rates and increasing the retention power of the school? (5) Which designs permit the greatest opportunities for alert students and reluctant learners? (6) Which design is most attractive to male teachers and heads of households? (7) Which designs provide maximum utilization of educational facilities and resources? (8) Which designs provide the greatest continuity of learning for students?

In spite of all our efforts directed toward the apparent issues, implications, and innuendos of the extended school year designs, we have come no closer to a resolution of many of the latter issues than our predecessors; and it is not likely that the efforts of our contemporaries nor our successors will be any more successful than the efforts of previous research scholars in year-round education.

There can never be an answer to all of the previous questions about the extended or year-round school concept that can be applied, in general, as an absolute to all of the extended school year or year-round designs currently in existence. Although some extended school year or year-round school designs were developed to resolve one particular school related problem in a community, several of the designs are known to possess the capability to resolve several school related problems in a community at the same time. If we place the length of the school year on a continuum from traditional or conventional to the flexible-all-year design, regardless of similarities among the programs, there are extreme variations within the administration and operation of the designs from one school corporation to another school corporation. This is definitely true with designs of different titles, which were developed to accomplish different purposes within a school system. It has been found to be equally as valid with some designs of the same title and similar structure.

Each extended school year design, in spite of the apparent similarities in school size, title, or structure, are as dissimilar in operation as school corporations conducted on a conventional school year schedule because of the many conscious and subconscious variables applied to each operation by administrators. I have heard it stated that school operations cannot be separate and equal or separate and identical. They may be separate and similar but not separate and identical even when the intent of school administrators is to make them exactly the same. If the previous assumptions are correct, it is as impossible to compare completely different extended school year or year-round programs as it is to compare the apple with the orange. Likewise, to compare designs that are apparently the same may be a frustrating and fruitless effort because what superficially appears to be the same or similar may be as different as the apple and the orange.

Each year-round school design was developed and selected to solve a specific set of objectives or to solve specific local school district problems. There was not enough commonality among year-round or extended school year designs or variations of the same year-round design to subject all extended school year or year-round designs to the scrutiny of an evaluation based upon a common set of objectives.

The most extensively used year-round school plan in the United States in 1973 was the Forty-Five—Fifteen design. All rotating-terms or cycle plans have objectives similar to the Forty-Five—Fifteen plan. The Flexible All-Year plan, the Continuous Four-Quarter plan, the Continuous School Year plan, Concept Six, and the Four-One-Four-One-One plan all provided varying degrees of flexibility in attendance and vacation patterns, educational opportunities, acceleration, and remediation of student progress, but were not designed to save money through the release of teacher time, classroom space or school facilities. All of the latter designs were operated at considerable additional cost to the taxpayers.

A majority of the community people in districts where year-round school plans were currently in operation or were to be implemented favored the year-round operation of schools, and in districts in which year-round plans were currently in operation, the community support for the program was increasing.

Comparative data on teacher preference for employment, student juvenile delinquency trends, vandalism, retention of cognitive materials, attendance rates, attrition rates, health, and achievement gave positive support to the value of year-round education. Extended school year programs did not, in general, prove to result in financial savings.

Year-round school operations were generally reported as a crisis innovation which occurred in times of high building costs, population increases, and tight economy. During periods of decrease in the population of the nation, the number of students served by the schools also decreases, and the year-round concept loses momentum.

If a revision of this book should ever be attempted, the topic should be approached by contrasting or by accentuating the differences between extended school year or year-round programs.

If you should ever have the opportunity to read or reread this account on the year-round concept, approach it with a contrasting, analytical mind, not a mind that wishes to compare. To compare extended school year programs or designs rather than to contrast them is to forever live with a repulsively asinine reluctance to extend the length of the school year.

Appendix A

ADMINISTRATIVE PROBLEMS RELATED TO EXTENDED SCHOOL YEAR OPERATIONS

ADMINISTRATIVE PROBLEMS REPORTED IN RANK ORDER OF IMPORTANCE
AND TABLED ACCORDING TO THE CURRENT STATUS OF THE EXTENDED YEAR PROGRAM

Responses	45-15 or 9-3	Flexible All-Year	Continuous School Year	Quadrimester	Quinmester or Pentamester	Continuous Four Quarter	Trimester	Concept Six	Extended K-12	60-20	Rotating Four Quarter	Other Variations	Total	Percentage of Total
Time for teachers involved in the program to attend school and gain professional growth	36	2	2	2	3	5	1	0	2	1	0	0	54	68.35
Conflicts between schedules of schools conducted on extended or year-round schedule and schools conducted on traditional schedule	25	1	1	1	4	3	1	0	1	1	0	0	38	48.10
Community opposition	25	1	1	2	1	3	1	0	1	1	1	0	37	46.84
Inadequate time for maintenance, renovation, clean-up work, and repairs	19	2	0	2	2	4	1	1	2	1	0	1	35	44.30
Teacher opposition	21	1	1	2	2	3	1	0	1	1	1	0	34	43.04
Inadequate funds for conducting extended session	14	1	2	1	2	9	1	1	2	0	0	1	34	43.04
Low attendance rate during summer months	9	2	1	1	3	6	1	1	2	1	1	0	28	35.44
Student opposition	15	1	0	2	1	3	1	0	1	1	1	0	26	32.91
Scheduling members of the same family in school during same term	18	2	0	1	1	2	1	0	0	1	0	0	26	32.91
Scheduling of student participants into extracurricular activities during terms when activities are in session	12	1	0	1	2	2	1	0	1	1	0	0	21	26.58
Scheduling an equal number of boys and girls into school each term	9	2	0	1	0	1	1	0	0	1	0	0	15	18.99

	1	2	3	4	5	6	7	8	9	10	11	12	13	No.	%
No response	1	0	0	1	0	0	1	0	0	0	0	4	0	7	8.86
Communication on extended school year concept with parents and teachers	1	0	1	0	0	0	0	0	0	0	0	0	0	2	2.53
Development of intersession curriculum	1	0	1	0	0	0	0	0	0	0	0	0	0	2	2.53
Development of ESY program suited to needs of community	1	0	1	0	0	0	0	0	0	0	0	0	0	2	2.53
Program is voluntary for teachers and students and ranking of administrative problems not applicable	0	0	0	1	0	1	0	0	0	0	0	0	0	2	2.53
Added operational cost	0	0	1	0	0	0	0	0	0	0	0	0	0	1	1.27
No vacation time for administration	0	1	0	0	0	0	0	0	0	0	0	0	0	1	1.27
Internal school scheduling	0	0	1	0	0	0	0	0	0	0	0	0	0	1	1.27
Community involvement in planning ESY program	1	0	0	0	0	0	0	0	0	0	0	0	0	1	1.27
District understanding of ESY program	1	0	0	0	0	0	0	0	0	0	0	0	0	1	1.27
Distribution of students to maintain a suitable balance of class size among the four attendance groups	1	0	0	0	0	0	0	0	0	0	0	0	0	1	1.27
Staff involvement in planning ESY program	1	0	0	0	0	0	0	0	0	0	0	0	0	1	1.27
Educating parents to the ESY philosophy	1	0	0	0	0	0	0	0	0	0	0	0	0	1	1.27
Student record keeping	0	0	0	1	0	0	0	0	0	0	0	0	0	1	1.27
Materials for new curriculum	0	0	0	1	0	0	0	0	0	0	0	0	0	1	1.27
Recruitment of staff for summer work	0	0	0	0	1	0	0	0	0	0	0	0	0	1	1.27
No problems existed that were the result of implementation of the program	0	1	0	0	0	0	0	0	0	0	0	0	0	1	1.27
None of the listed problems existed in the district	0	0	0	0	1	0	0	0	0	0	0	0	0	1	1.27

*Seventy-nine responding school officials represent 100 percent of the total study population, and the total population could have responded to any one or all of the administrative problems listed in this table. As a result, the total number of school officials responding to each administrative problem listed in this table represents a number and percentage of the total study population of seventy-nine officials. The percentage figures are also based upon seventy-nine as 100 percent of the study population in each case. The total number of respondents to each administrative problem and the percentage of respondents are treated as separate entities from each of the other administrative problems listed. Each administrative problem is based upon the possibility of responses from seventy-nine (100%) of the total study population.

Appendix B

RATIONALE FOR IMPLEMENTATION OF THE EXTENDED SCHOOL YEAR

RESPONSES ON RATIONALE FOR IMPLEMENTATION OF EXTENDED SCHOOL YEAR PROGRAMS

Responses	45-15 or 9-3	Flexible All-Year	Continuous School Year	Quadrimester	Quinmester or Pentamester	Continuous Four Quarter	Trimester	Concept Six	Extended K-12	60-20	Rotating Four Quarter	Other Variations	Total*	Percentage of Total*
Make better utilization of costly plant facilities largely unused or underused during three months of summer	28	1	2	2	6	10	0	2	2	1	1	1	56	71
Improve and reorganize the curriculum	20	3	3	1	7	10	1	1	1	1	1	1	50	63
To add enrichment courses to the curriculum	13	2	2	2	6	11	1	2	2	0	1	1	43	54
Prevent loss of learning during summer vacation	21	2	3	2	0	4	1	2	2	1	0	0	38	48
Save money by reducing the number of school plants and facilities needed	18	0	1	1	3	4	1	1	0	1	1	0	31	39
Make better utilization of the time of pupils during the summer months, reducing juvenile delinquency	11	2	2	1	2	6	1	0	0	1	1	1	28	35
Conduct experiments on the total effects of year-round or extended school year programs	10	2	1	1	5	5	0	0	1	1	1	1	28	35
Save money by delaying construction costs and thus eliminating need to ask taxpayers to support bond issues	17	0	1	1	1	3	1	0	0	0	1	0	25	32

Rationale for implementation													Number	Percent
Reduce the student dropout rate	3	1	1	1	6	6	1	1	2	0	1	1	24	30
To provide a solution to crowded conditions while needed buildings were being completed	15	0	1	0	2	1	1	1	0	1	0	0	22	28
To help reluctant learners catch up	2	2	2	0	1	7	1	1	2	0	0	1	19	24
Give teachers employment during the summer months thus increasing teacher salaries and professional status	5	0	3	0	3	3	0	2	0	1	0	1	18	23
Save money by reducing the number of pupils who were required to repeat a grade, reducing enrollment	4	0	1	0	3	3	0	0	1	0	0	0	12	15
Save money by permitting the acceleration of bright pupils resulting in savings of years of schooling per accelerated pupil	1	0	2	0	4	2	0	0	1	0	0	0	10	13
Make teaching in district more attractive to men through greater earning possibilities	3	0	1	0	2	1	0	0	0	1	0	0	8	10
No response	1	0	0	0	0	0	1	0	0	0	4	0	6	8
Force community to provide needed funds for school construction	0	0	0	0	2	1	0	0	1	0	0	0	4	5
Improve education opportunities	1	0	0	0	0	0	0	0	0	0	0	0	1	1
Acquire needed space	1	0	0	0	0	0	0	0	0	0	0	0	1	1
Meet increasing enrollment	0	0	0	1	0	0	0	0	0	0	0	0	1	1
To improve educational achievement	0	0	0	0	0	0	0	0	0	0	0	1	1	1
To eliminate double sessions	1	0	0	0	0	0	0	0	0	0	0	0	1	1
To give students more options	0	0	0	0	1	0	0	0	0	0	0	0	1	1

*Seventy-nine responding school officials represented 100 percent of the total study population and the total population could have responded to any one or all of the rationale for implementation listed in this table. As a result, the total number of respondants to each rationale for implementation and the percentage of respondants are treated as separate entities from each of the other rationale for implementation herein listed. Each item is based upon the possible response of school officials who represent seventy-nine (100%) of the total study population. The total number of school officials responding to each rationale for implementation listed in this table represents a number and a percentage of the total study population of seventy-nine school officials.

Appendix C

MOST SIGNIFICANT RATIONALE FOR IMPLEMENTATION
OF EXTENDED SCHOOL YEAR PROGRAMS

Responses	45-15 or 9-3	Flexible All-Year	Continuous School Year	Quadrimester	Quinmester or Pentamester	Continuous Four Quarter	Trimester	Concept Six	Extended K-12	60-20	Rotating Four Quarter	Other Variations	Total	Percentage of Total
Improve and reorganize the curriculum	10	2	1	0	5	7	0	1	2	0	0	1	29	37
Make better utilization of costly plant facilities largely unused or underused during three months of summer	15	0	1	1	2	2	0	2	2	1	0	1	27	34
To add enrichment courses to the curriculum	7	1	2	1	3	3	0	0	0	0	0	1	18	23
To provide a solution to crowded conditions while needed buildings were being completed	12	0	1	0	0	0	0	0	0	1	0	0	14	18
Prevent loss of learning during summer vacation	6	1	2	1	1	2	0	0	0	0	0	0	13	16
Save money by reducing the number of school plants and facilities needed	8	0	1	2	0	0	0	0	0	0	0	0	11	14
Save money by delaying construction costs and thus eliminating need to ask taxpayers to support bond issues	9	0	0	0	0	1	1	0	0	0	0	0	10	13
No response	2	0	0	0	1	0	1	0	0	0	1	4	9	11
Help disadvantaged catch up	0	1	1	0	0	2	0	0	2	0	0	0	6	8

Rationale for implementation														No.	%
Save money by reducing number of pupils who were required to repeat a grade, reducing enrollment	0	0	1	0	1	1	0	0	2	0	0	0	0	5	6
Make better utilization of the time of pupils during the summer months, reducing juvenile delinquency	2	0	1	0	0	0	0	0	0	0	0	0	1	4	5
Conduct experiments on the effects of year-round or extended school year programs	0	0	1	0	1	1	0	0	1	0	0	0	0	4	5
Give teachers employment during the summer months thus increasing teacher salaries and professional status	1	0	0	0	3	0	0	0	0	0	0	0	0	4	5
Save money by permitting the acceleration of bright pupils resulting in savings of years of schooling per accelerated pupil	1	0	1	0	1	0	0	0	0	0	0	0	0	3	4
Make teaching in district more attractive to men through greater earning possibilities	0	0	0	0	2	0	0	0	0	0	0	0	0	2	3
Reduce the dropout rate	0	0	0	0	2	0	0	0	0	0	0	0	0	2	3
Meet increasing enrollment	1	0	0	0	0	0	1	0	0	0	0	0	0	2	3
To improve academic achievement	1	0	0	1	0	0	0	0	0	0	0	0	0	2	3
Improve education opportunities	1	0	0	0	0	0	0	0	0	0	0	0	0	1	1
Acquire needed space	1	0	0	0	0	0	0	0	0	0	0	0	0	1	1
Force community to provide needed funds for school construction	0	0	0	0	1	0	0	0	0	0	0	0	0	1	1
To give students more options	0	0	0	0	1	0	0	0	0	0	0	0	0	1	1

*Seventy-nine responding school officials represented 100 percent of the total study population and the total population could have responded to any one or all of the rationale for implementation listed in this table. As a result, the total number of respondants to each rationale for implementation and the percentage of respondants are treated as separate entities from each of the other rationale for implementation herein listed. Each item is based upon the possible response of school officials who represent seventy-nine (100%) of the total study population. The total number of school officials responding to each rationale for implementation listed in this table represents a number and a percentage of the total study population of seventy-nine school officials.

Appendix D

SURVEY INSTRUMENT TWO

Name of Responding Official: _____
Official Title: _____
City: _____
School District: _____
State: _____

Please complete the questionnaire by placing a check ( ) in the appropriate place and/or completing the blank space beside the statement which most accurately describes the year-round or extended school year program in the district. Please respond to all applicable items.

1. An extended or year-round school program is currently in operation in the school district. (Please indicate year of implementation.)   ( )   19__

2. An extended or year-round school program is to be implemented in the district in the near future. (If the plan is to be implemented, please indicate when and answer all of the remaining questions where possible.)   ( )   197__

3. The extended or year-round program has been abandoned in the district. (Specify when.)   ( )   19__

4. Check the type of year-round or extended school year program currently in operation, to be implemented, or abandoned in the district:

    A. Quadrimester   ( )

    B. Continuous Four-Quarter   ( )

    C. Trimester   ( )

    D. Split Trimester   ( )

    E. Quinmester   ( )

    F. Continuous School Year   ( )

    G. Extended K-12 Plan   ( )

    H. Extended or Modified Summer School   ( )

    I. Multiple Trails   ( )

    J. Flexible All-Year School   ( )

    K. Rotating Four-Quarter   ( )

    L. Compulsory Four-Quarter for All   ( )

    M. Rotating Trimester   ( )

    N. Rotating-Term or Cycle Plan   ( )

        (1) Forty-Five—Fifteen   ( )

        (2) Nine-Three   ( )

        (3) Twelve-Four   ( )

(4) Eight-Two   ( )

(5) Others (please specify) _____

O. Conventional Summer School   ( )

P. Other Types (please specify) _____

5. Did the district implement one type of extended or year-round plan and later change to a different type? (If so, please indicate previous type plan.)

Yes ( )   No ( )

6. Total number of days of instruction in the school year.

7. Minimum number of days of attendance required by law for each pupil.

8. Number of days of instruction in each term or division of the year.

9. Length of the school day in schools operating on an extended or year-round basis.

10. Number of days of instruction per week in year-round or extended schools.

11. Total number of public schools in the school district.

   A. Elementary _____
   B. Middle Schools _____
   C. Junior High Schools _____
   D. High Schools _____

12. Total number of public schools involved in the extended or year-round operation:

   A. Elementary _____
   B. Middle School _____
   C. Junior High Schools _____
   D. High Schools _____

13. Total student population in public schools in the district.

14. Total student population in public schools involved in the extended or year-round operation.

15. Total number of teachers in the district.

16. Total number of teachers in the district who are heads of households.

17. Total number of teachers in the district who teach on year-round or extended year contracts (not the teachers who have nine-month salaries paid in extended installments).

18. Total number of teachers who are heads of households who teach on a year-round or extended school year contract.

---

19. Total number of classroom teachers in the district who are men.

---

20. Total number of men teachers who teach on year-round or extended school year contracts.

---

21. The percentage of increase in the number of male teachers working in extended or year-round programs since implementation.   %_____

22. Do new teacher applicants to the district or request from teachers already in the district indicate that heads of households perfer working in the extended or year-round programs because of increased earning possibilities?
                                                        Yes( )   No( )

23. Do new teacher applications from men or requests from men teachers already in the district indicate that men teachers prefer working in the extended or year-round school program because of increased earning possibilities?
                                                        Yes( )   No( )

24. Source of funding for the extended or year-round operations is:

    A. Federal funds only (special grant)   ( )

    B. Federal funds (ESEA Title III)   ( )

    C. Local tax levies   ( )

    D. Private foundation   ( )

    E. Student tuition   ( )

    F. Regular state allocation   ( )

    G. A combination of the above. (Specify the combination, A & B, etc.) _____

25. Are there state laws which restrict any or all year-round or extended school year operations (check all applicable boxes)?   Yes( )   No( )

    A. Minimum number of days for school operation (if applicable, indicate number). #_____   Yes( )   No( )

    B. Maximum number of days for school operation (if applicable, indicate number).   ( )   #_____

    C. State allocations based on ADA (Average Daily Attendance).
                                                             ( )

    D. State Allocations based on ADM (Average Daily Membership).
                                                             ( )

    E. Maximum number of days or months for which teachers may be paid (if applicable, indicate number).   ( )   #_____

    F. State allocations based on a factor-number of students in attendance during a specific period in the school year (for example, allocations based on the number of students enrolled during the first 20 days of the school year).   ( )

    G. Others (please specify). _____

26. Have state laws been passed which aid district officials in the implementation of extended or year-round programs?   Yes( )   No( )

27. If state laws have been passed, did the laws favor a particular type of extended or year-round plan?   Yes( )   No( )

28. If the answer to number 27 is "yes", please specify the type of plan favored by the legislation.   _____

29. Check each rationale for implementation listed below which caused district officials to implement an extended or year-round program:

    A. To save money by reducing the number of school plant and facilities needed.   ( )

    B. To save money by delaying construction cost and thus eliminating the need to ask taxpayers to support bond issues.   ( )

    C. To save money by permitting the acceleration of bright pupils resulting in a savings of one or two years of schooling per accelerated pupil.   ( )

    D. To save money by reducing the number of pupils who are required to repeat a grade thereby reducing enrollment.   ( )

    E. To make better utilization of costly plant facilities which were largely unused or underused during the three months of the summer.   ( )

    F. To make better utilization of the time of pupils during the summer months thereby reducing juvenile delinquency.   ( )

    G. To provide enrichment courses to the curriculum.   ( )

    H. To reduce the dropout rate.   ( )

    I. To improve and reorganize the curriculum.   ( )

    J. To force the community to provide needed funds for school construction, etc.   ( )

    K. To help the disadvantaged catch up.   ( )

    L. To prevent the loss of learning during the summer vacations.   ( )

    M. To give teachers employment during the summer months thus increasing teacher salaries and professional status.   ( )

    N. To make teaching in the district more attractive to men through greater earning possibilities.   ( )

    O. To provide a solution to crowded conditions while needed buildings were being completed.   ( )

    P. To conduct experiments on the effects of year-round or extended year school programs.   ( )

30. Which reason or reasons for implementation previously mentioned were most significant in the decision of school officials to implement an extended or year-round program. (Please indicate by the alphabets before the rationale.)

    _____

31. Rank each administrative problem from 1-11 using one to indicate the greatest problem, two as the second greatest problem, and 11 as the problem of least magnitude. Use an X to indicate the items which are not considered problems in the district.

    A. Community opposition   ( )

    B. Teacher opposition   ( )

    C. Student opposition   ( )

D. Time for teachers involved in the program to attend school and gain professional growth.   ( )

E. Scheduling members of the same family in school during the same terms.   ( )

F. Scheduling an "equal" number of boys and girls in school each term.   ( )

G. Low attendance rate during the summer months.   ( )

H. Scheduling of all student participants in extracurricular activities during the terms when such activities are in session.   ( )

I. Inadequate time for maintenance renovations, clean-up work, and repairs.   ( )

J. Inadequate funds for operating the extended session.   ( )

K. Conflicts between the schedules of schools operating on an extended or year-round schedule and schools which do not (children transferring from an extended concept school to a conventional school or members of the same family in the two different type schools).   ( )

L. Others (please specify) _____

32. Did the *total* expenditures for the district in the school or schools where the extended or year-round school program was implemented decrease or increase after implementation excluding normal increases in salaries, etc? (Indicate the percentage of increase or decrease.)

Increased ( ) %_____   Decreased ( ) %_____

33. Would the total projected expenditures have increased more than the cost of operating an extended year plan in the extended year schools had the plan not been implemented? (Indicate percentage.)

Increased ( ) %_____   Decreased ( ) %_____   No change ( )

34. Did implementation of the plan provide officials a means of solving a local problem without raising the local tax rate or using local funds?

Yes ( )   No ( )

35. Was the plan implemented because the community had rejected a local bond issue which necessitated the implementation of some innovation to solve the problems?

Yes ( )   No ( )

36. Was the district at the legal maximum bonded indebtedness when the plan was implemented?

Yes ( )   No ( )

37. Would district officials have attempted a year-round or extended year program if outside sources of funds could not have been acquired for implementation?

Yes ( )   No ( )

38. Is the plan likely to be continued after the situations which caused implementation have been resolved?

Yes ( )   No ( )

39. Was the plan implemented in spite of opposition by a majority of community people?

Yes ( )   No ( )

40. What percentage of the community people supported the year-round or extended year concept before implementation?

%_____

41. What percentage of the community people support the operation now? _____

42. Has juvenile delinquency increased or decreased among students who participate in year-round or extended year programs? (Please indicate percentage of increase or decrease.)

Increased ( ) %_____   Decreased ( ) %_____

43. Do students who attend conventional schools have a higher or lower delinquency rate than students who attend year-round or extended year programs?

Higher ( )   Lower ( )   No Difference ( )

44. Has school vandalism decreased or increased in the schools operating on an extended or year-round basis?

Decreased ( )   Increased ( )   No Change ( )

45. Does more or less school vandalism occur in conventional schools than in schools of the district operating on a year-round or extended concept?

More ( )   Less ( )   No Difference ( )

46. Has the dropout rate increased or decreased in schools where year-round or extended school year programs are in operation since implementation?

Increased ( )   Decreased ( )   No Change ( )

47. Is the dropout rate higher or lower in conventional schools than in year-round or extended year schools?

Higher ( )   Lower ( )   No Difference ( )

48. Is the attendance rate of students in the school or schools where the year-round or extended concept was implemented higher or lower since implementation? (Indicate percentage.)

Higher ( )   Lower ( )   Average Daily
Attendance Now _____
Average Daily
Attendance
before Imple-
mentation _____

49. Is the attendance rate of students in the conventional school higher or lower than students in year-round or extended school year programs?

Higher ( )   Lower ( )   No Difference ( )
Average Daily
Attendance
Conventional
Schools _____

50. How does the average daily attendance rate during the summer session compare with other sessions of the year—higher or lower?

Higher ( )   Lower ( )   No Difference ( )

51. What percentage of the students involved in year-round or extended year programs have been able to accelerate toward graduation by one, two or three years?

One Year %_____   Two Years %_____   Three Years %_____

52. What percentage of the students involved in the year-round or extended year program have been able to avoid repeating a grade by using the summers for make-up?   %_____

53. Has the year-round or extended operation had a negative or positive effect on the health of students who attend year-round or extended year schools?

    Positive( )   Negative( )   No Effect( )

54. Has the year-round or extended operation had a positive or negative effect on the achievement of the students who attend school year-round or on an extended basis as measured by standardized test and grades?

    Positive( )   Negative( )   No Effect( )

55. As measured by standardized test and grades, has the year-round or extended operation had a positive or negative effect on achievement of students of the same age, sex and I.Q. who attend school on an extended basis as compared to students in conventional schools?

    Positive( )   Negative( )   No Effect( )

56. Does attending school without the long vacation seem to have a positive effect on the retention rate of students (less loss of learning)?

    Yes( )   No( )

57. What is the maximum number of new courses added to the curriculum of a year-round or extended year school since the implementation?

    #_____

58. Had the conditions surrounding implementation of the year-round or extended year concept not existed, would district officials have implemented the plan for other educationally sound reasons?

    Yes( )   No)

59. Was the plan implemented with full commitment for continued operation or was the plan a pilot or experimental program?

    Full Commitment( )   Pilot or Experimental( )

60. Did projected enrollment figures suggest that a year-round or extended year plan could temporarily solve the problems of the district and eliminate the need for new buildings in the future?

    Yes( )   No( )

61. What percentage of teachers, facilities and classroom space were freed for other use as a result of implementation?   %_____

62. Do the standardized test scores of pupils who attend school on an extended or year-round basis indicate an educational *gain* on students of the same sex and age with higher I.Q. scores who attend conventional schools?

    Yes( )   No( )

63. Did the district officials have to air-condition building for use during the summer months?

    Yes( )   No( )

64. Has the district experienced more resignations or requests for transfers from teachers who work in extended school year programs?

    Yes( )   No( )

65. Comments:

Appendix E

CURRENTLY OPERATING EXTENDED SCHOOL PLANS

Arizona

*Dr. George Smith, Superintendent
Mesa District #4
549 N. Stapley
Mesa, Arizona 85203

*Mr. Ira A. Murphy, Superintendent
Peoria District #11
11150 N. 83rd Avenue
Peoria, Arizona 85345

Mr. Willard A. Canode, Superintendent
Yuma Union High School District #7
400 6th Avenue
Yuma, Arizona 85364
(Continuous Four-Quarter)

California

Mr. Charles W. L. Hutchinson,
  Superintendent
A B C Unified School District
17923 S. Pioneer Boulevard
Artesia, California 90701
(Furgeson Flexible All Year Plan
of Continuous Progress)

*Mr. Ralph R. Bell, Superintendent
Bear Valley Unified School District
41220 Park Avenue (P. O. Box 1529)
Big Bear Lake, California 92315
(to change from Forty-Five—Fifteen
to Rotating Four-Quarter)

Mr. F. Gregory Betts, Superintendent
Berryessa Union School District
935 Piedmont Road
San Jose, California 95132
(Forty-Five—Fifteen)

Mr. Charles S. Terrell, Jr.
  Superintendent
Corona-Norco Unified School District
300 Buena Vista Avenue
Corona, California 91720
(Forty-Five—Fifteen)

Mr. James M. Slezak, Superintendent
Escondido City Elementary School
District
Fifth and Maple Streets
Escondido, California 92025
(Forty-Five—Fifteen)

Mr. Raymond G. Arveson,
  Superintendent
Hayward Unified School District
1099 "E" Street (P. O. Box 5000)
Hayward, California 94541
(Continuous Four-Quarter)

Mr. Howard A. Carmichael,
  Superintendent
Hesperia Elementary School District
16079 Main Street
Hesperia, California 92345
(Forty-Five—Fifteen)

Mr. Roy C. Hill, Superintendent
San Bernardino County School District
Juniper School
Hesperia, California 92345
(Forty-Five—Fifteen)

Mr. Burton C. Tiffany, Superintendent
Chula Vista City School District
84 E. J. Street
Chula Vista, California 92012
(Forty-Five—Fifteen)

133

Mr. James R. Carvell, Superintendent
Ocean View Elementary School
District
7972 Warner Avenue
Huntington Beach, California 92647
(Forty-Five—Fifteen)

Mr. Lesly Meyer, Superintendent
Petaluma City Elementary School
District
11 Fifth Street
Petaluma, California 94952
(Forty-Five—Fifteen)

Mr. Dean Magowan, Superintendent
Old Adobe Union Elementary School
District
1600 Albin Way
Petaluma, California 94952
(Forty-Five—Fifteen)

Mr. John W. Duncan, Superintendent
Pajaro Valley Joint Unified School
District
165 Blackburn Street (P. O. Box 630)
Watsonville, California 95076
(Forty-Five—Fifteen)

Mr. Thomas L. Goodman,
  Superintendent
San Diego City Unified School District
4100 Normal Street
San Diego, California 92103
(Forty-Five—Fifteen)

Mr. Ralph A. Gates, Superintendent
San Joaquin Elementary School District
14600 Sand Canyon Avenue (P. O. Box
92)
East Irvine, California 92650
(Forty-Five—Fifteen)

Mr. Charles E. Skidmore,
  Superintendent
Santee Elementary School District
9625 Cuyamaca Street (P. O. Box 220)
Santee, California 92071
(Forty-Five—Fifteen)

Mr. Michael Brick, Superintendent
Fountain Valley Elementary School
District
Number One Lighthouse Lane
Fountain Valley, California 92708
(Forty-Five—Fifteen and
  Quadrimester)

Mr. Robert D. Muscio, Superintendent
Lakeside Union Elementary School
District
12335 Woodside Avenue (P. O. Box 578)
Lakeside, California 92040
(Forty-Five—Fifteen)

Mr. James R. Runge, Superintendent
LaMesa-Spring Valley Elementary
School District
4750 Date Avenue
LaMesa, California 92041
(Forty-Five—Fifteen)

Colorado

Dr. Richard Koeppe, Superintendent
Cherry Creek School District #5
4700 So. Yosemite
Englewood, Colorado 80110
(Forty-Five—Fifteen)

Florida

Mr. Warren C. Smith, Superintendent
Nova Schools
Fort Lauderdale, Florida 33314
(Extended K-Twelve)

Dr. E. L. Whigham, Superintendent
Dade County School Board
1410 N. E. Second Avenue
Miami, Florida 33132
(Quinmester)

Dr. Wayne H. White, Superintendent
Brevard County Schools
Titusville, Florida 32780
(Forty-Five—Fifteen)

Dr. Mary Zellner, Principal
S. Bryan Gennings Elementary School
Orange Park (Clay County), Florida
32073
(Continuous School Year)

*Mr. Ralph L. Witherspoon, Director
Laboratory School
Florida State University
Tallahassee, Florida

Mr. James K. Austin, Superintendent
Hernando County School Board
612 West Broad Street
Brooksville, Florida 33512
(Continuous Four-Quarter and
Extended K-Twelve)

Georgia

Dr. John Letson, Superintendent
Atlanta City Schools
224 Central Avenue
Atlanta, Georgia 30303
(Continuous Four-Quarter)

Illinois

Mr. James F. Redmond,
  Superintendent
City of Chicago School District #299
228 N. La Salle Street
Chicago, Illinois 60601
(Forty-Five—Fifteen)

Mr. Kenneth Hermanser,
  Superintendent
Valley View C. U. 365
104 McKool Avenue
Lockport, Illinois
(Forty-Five—Fifteen)

Kansas

Mr. Arzel L. Ball, Superintendent
Shawnee Mission Northwest
12701 W. 67th.
Shawnee Mission, Kansas 66316

Kentucky

Dr. Richard VanHoose, Superintendent
Jefferson County School District
3332 Newburg Road
Louisville, Kentucky
(Continuous Four-Quarter)

Michigan

Mr. Malcolm Katz, Superintendent
East Lansing Public Schools
509 Burcham Drive
East Lansing, Michigan
(Quinmester)

Mr. Raymond E. Spear, Superintendent
Northville Public Schools
303 West Main Street
Northville, Michigan
(Forty-Five—Fifteen)

Minnesota

Mr. Pius Lacher, Superintendent
Mora Public Schools
400 E. Maple Street
Mora, Minnesota 55051
(Forty-Five—Fifteen)

Dr. Joseph Schulze, Director
Wilson Campus School
Mankato State College
Mankato, Minnesota 56001
(Quinmester)

Missouri

Dr. M. G. Henderson, Superintendent
Francis Howell R-III
Route 2
St. Charles, Missouri 63301
(Nine-Three)

Nevada

*Dr. Marvin Piccolo, Superintendent
Washoe County Schools
Reno, Nevada 89501

New Hampshire

Mr. Peter G. Dolloff, Superintendent
Hudson, Alvirne High School District
Thorning Road
Hudson, New Hampshire 03051
(Continuous Four-Quarter)

New York

Dr. Samuel Ross, Jr., Headmaster
Green Chimney School
Brewster, New York 10509
(Continuous School Year)

North Carolina

Mr. Fred Martin, Superintendent
Buncombe County Schools
P. O. Box 7557
Asheville, North Carolina 28807
(Continuous Four-Quarter)

Mr. Marvin Ward, Superintendent
Winston-Salem/Forsyth School
P. O. Box 2513
Winston-Salem, North Carolina 27102
(Forty-Five—Fifteen)

Oregon

Mr. William Jordan, Superintendent
Molalla Elementary School District #35
P. O. Box 107
Molalla, Oregon 97038
(Abandoning Forty-Five—Fifteen to
implement Continuous Four-Quarter)

Mr. Gordon Russell, Superintendent
Gresham School District #4
1400 S. E. Fifth
Gresham, Oregon 97030
(Forty-Five—Fifteen)

Pennsylvania

Mr. Matthew Hosie, Superintendent
Rochester Area School District
540 Reno Street
Rochester, Pennsylvania
(Continuous Four-Quarter)

Texas

Mr. George G. Carver, Superintendent
Houston Independent School District
3830 Richmond Ave.
Houston, Texas 77027
(Trimester)

Mr. Joe R. Sherrod
Special Assistant to the Superintendent
Fort Worth Independent School District
3210 West Lancaster
Fort Worth, Texas 76107
(Trimester)

Utah

Mr. Royal N. Allred, Superintendent
North Sanpete School District
Mt. Pleasant, Utah 84647
(Continuous Four-Quarter)

Dr. Joe A. Reidhead, Superintendent
Nebo School District
Spanish Fork, Utah 84660
(Continuous School Year)

Vermont

Mr. John Olsen, Principal
Champlain Valley Union High School
Hinesburg, Vermont 05461
(Forty-Five—Fifteen)

Virginia

Mr. Herbert J. Saunders,
  Superintendent
Prince William County School District
Box 389
Manassas, Virginia 22110
(Forty-Five—Fifteen)

West Virginia

*Mr. Howard Charlton, Principal
Fairmont Senior High School
Loop Park Drive
Fairmont, West Virginia 26554

*Mr. T. J. Hardin, Jr., Principal
Kermit High School
Kermit, West Virginia 25674

*Mr. A. R. Marushi, Principal
Logan High School
P. O. Box 1271
Logan, West Virginia 25601

*Mr. Ray Waldo, Jr., Principal
Martinsburg High School
Buxton Street
Martinsburg, West Virginia 25401

*Mr. George S. Mullett, Principal
Magnolia High School
Maple Avenue
New Martinsville, West Virginia 26155

*Pineville High School
Drawer O
Pineville, West Virginia 24874

*Mr. Robert L. Turner, Principal
Big Creek High School
Box 278
War, West Virginia 24892

*Mr. Harry Hatfield, Principal
Williamson High School
Williamson, West Virginia 25661

Washington

Dr. Ed Hill, Superintendent
Franklin-Pierce School District #402
315 South 129th Street
Tacoma, Washington 98444
(Four-One-Four-One-One)

*School districts in which officials were identified as currently operating an extended or year-round program, but the status of the district operation was not determined.

Appendix F

EXTENDED SCHOOL YEAR PLANS
TO BE IMPLEMENTED

Arizona

Dr. Thomas Reno, Superintendent
Apache Junction High School District
#843
P. O. Box 879
Apache Junction, Arizona 85220
(Forty-Five—Fifteen)

Mr. Don L. Wagner, Superintendent
Buckeye District #33
210 S. 6th Street
Buckeye, Arizona 85326
(Forty-Five—Fifteen)

Dr. Gerald DeGrow, Superintendent
Phœnix Union High School District
#210
2526 W. Osborn Road
Phoenix, Arizona 85017
(Rotating Four-Quarter)

Dr. Russell Jackson, Superintendent
Roosevelt District #66
6000 S. 7th Street
Phoenix, Arizona 85040
(Forty-Five—Fifteen)

Dr. Gabriel Reuben, Superintendent
Scottsdale High School District #212
3811 N. 44th Street
Phoenix, Arizona 85018
(Forty-Five—Fifteen)

Dr. Pat B. Henderson, Superintendent
Sunnyside High School District #12
470 E. Valencia Road
Tucson, Arizona 85706
(Forty-Five—Fifteen)

California

*Mr. H. Lawson Smith, Superintendent
Chico Unified School District
1163 E. Seventh Street
Chico, California 95926

*Mr. Vincent Alexander,
    Superintendent
Culver City Unified School District
4534 Irving Place
Culver City, California 90230

Mr. Warren Linville, Superintendent
San Ramon Valley Unified School
District
699 Old Orchard Drive
Danville, California 94526
(Twelve-Four Trimester)

Mr. Lewis J. Ferrari, Superintendent
Marysville Joint Unified School District
504 J Street
Maryville, California 95901
(Forty-Five—Fifteen)

Mr. Edward C. Bates, Superintendent
Milpitas Unified School District
1500 Escuela Parkway
Milpitas, California 95035
(Forty-Five—Fifteen)

*Mr. Arthur Doornbos, Superintendent
Timber Elementary School District
1872 Newbury Road
Newbury Park, California 91320

138

Mr. Marcus A. Foster, Superintendent
Oakland City Unified School District
1025 Second Avenue
Oakland, California 94606
(Forty-Five—Fifteen)

Colorado

Mr. Tom Doherty, Superintendent
El Paso County #11
1115 N. El Paso
Colorado Springs, Colorado
(Concept-Six)

Dr. Alton W. Cowan, Superintendent
Jefferson County School District #1
3115 South Kipling
Morrison, Colorado 80465
(Concept-Six)

Michigan

Mr. George B. Glinke, Director of Year
   Round Education
Utica Community School District
Utica, Michigan 48087
(Quadrimester)

Montana

Mr. George M. Zellick, Superintendent
Missoula County High School
c/o Missoula Public Schools
Missoula, Montana 59801
(Quinmester)

New Hampshire

Mr. John W. Day, Superintendent
Keene School District
1 Elm Street
Keene, New Hampshire 03431
(Continuous Four-Quarter)

Ohio

Mr. Harold E. Schnell, Superintendent
West Carrollton City Schools
430 E. Pease Avenue
West Carrollton, Ohio 45400
(Nine-Three)

Pennsylvania

Mr. Samuel DeSimone, Acting
   Superintendent
Butler Area School District
167 New Castle Road
Butler, Pennsylvania 16001
(Continuous Four-Quarter)

Dr. John McLain, Director
Becker Research Learning Center
Clarion State College
Clarion, Pennsylvania 16214
(Flexible All-Year)

Rhode Island

*Mr. Curtis F. Bumpus, Superintendent
Foster-Glocester School District
R. D. 2
North Scituate, Rhode Island 02857

South Carolina

Mr. Joe Gentry, Superintendent
Piedmont Schools Project
206 Church Street
Greer, South Carolina 29651
(Quinmester)

Mr. B. J. Savage, Jr.
Rock Hill School District #3
522 East Main
Rock Hill, South Carolina 29730
(Quinmester)

Mr. J. G. McCracken, Superintendent
Spartanburg School District #7
Dupre Drive
Spartanburg, South Carolina 29300
(Quinmester)

Virginia

Mr. Robert E. Butt, Superintendent
Loudoun County School District
School Board Annex
30 West North Street
Leesburg, Virginia 22075
(Forty-Five—Fifteen)

Mr. L. D. Adams, Superintendent
Richmond City School District
Northside Middle School
4011 Moss Side Street
Richmond, Virginia 23222
(Flexible All-Year)

Mr. G. H. Pope, Superintendent
York County Public Schools
P. O. Box 451
Yorktown, Virginia 23490
(Quinmester)

Mr. Arnold R. Burton, Superintendent
Roanoke County School District
526 College Avenue
Salem, Virginia 24153
(Continuous School Year)

Mr. E. E. Brickell, Superintendent
Virginia Beach City School District
Annex 4
Virginia Beach, Virginia 23456
(Forty-Five—Fifteen)

*School Districts in which officials were identified as contemplating implementation of an extended school year, but the investigation failed to determine the district status on the extended year concept.

Appendix G

ABANDONED EXTENDED SCHOOL YEAR PLANS

California

Mr. Fred Kiesel, Superintendent
San Juan Unified School District
3738 Walnut Avenue
Carmichael, California 95608
(PACE—Personalized Accelerated
Curriculum Experiment)

Colorado

Dr. E. F. Clemmer, Superintendent
Widefield-Security School District
701 Widefield Drive
Security, Colorado 80911
(Unknown)

Florida

Mr. Thomas L. Casey, Superintendent
Bradford County Schools
Drawer 939
Starke, Florida
(Extended K-Twelve)

Hawaii

Officials in the state of Hawaii, having a state school system, conducted a state feasibility study on the extended school year and implemented a pilot program in the Kona Schools. The pilot program has since been abandoned.

New York

All experimental programs in the extended or year-round concept were abandoned.

South Dakota

Mr. Morris Magnosen, Superintendent
Brandon Valley Schools
201 W. 38th Street
Brandon Valley, South Dakota
(Forty-Five—Fifteen)

West Virginia

Mr. John T. Grossi, Night School
   Principal
Weir High School
Sinclair Avenue
Weirton, West Virginia 26062
(Unknown)

141

Appendix H

EXTENDED SCHOOL FEASIBILITY STUDIES
CONDUCTED SINCE 1968

Alaska

Dr. Cliff R. Hartman, Ass't.
  Superintendent
Anchorage Borough Schools
670 Fireweed Lane
Anchorage, Alaska 99503

California

Mr. Glenn R. Houde, Superintendent
Elk Grove Unified School District
Elk Grove, California 92624

Mr. William J. Bolt, Superintendent
Fremont Unified School District
40775 Fremont Blvd.
Fremont, California 94538

Mr. Eugene B. Even, Superintendent
Paradise Unified School District
728 Fir Street
Paradise, California 95969

Mr. John Reinking, Superintendent
Rose City Elementary School District
200 Branstetter Street
Roseville, California 95678

Mr. Charles S. Knight, Superintendent
San Jose Unified School District
1605 Park Avenue
San Jose, California 95114

Colorado

Dr. Barnard D. Ryan, Superintendent
Boulder Valley School District
Boulder County No. RE-2
6500 East Arapahoe Road
Boulder, Colorado 80302

Dr. George W. Bailey, Superintendent
East Lake School District
Adams County No. 12
10280 North Huron Street
Denver, Colorado 80221

Florida

Mr. Chester W. Taylor, Jr.,
  Superintendent
Pasco County School Board
115 County Courthouse
Dade City, Florida 33525

Mr. Ray Williams, Superintendent
Lee County School Board
Lee County Courthouse
Fort Myers, Florida 33901

Mr. Jesse Tynes, Jr., Superintendent
Clay County School Board
Box 488
Green Cove Springs, Florida 32043

Mr. John Columbo, Superintendent
Osceola County School Board
P. O. Box 939
Kissimmee, Florida 32741

Dr. Donald Ney, Superintendent
Orange County School Board
P. O. Box 271
Orlando, Florida 32802

Mr. John F. Gaines, Superintendent
Putnam County School Board
P. O. Box 797
Palatka, Florida 32077

Mr. John Angel, Superintendent
Seminole County School Board
202 Commercial Avenue
Sanford, Florida 32771

Mr. Freeman Ashmore, Superintendent
Leon County School Board
P. O. Box 246
Tallahassee, Florida 32302

Idaho

Dr. Stephenson Youngerman,
    Superintendent
Independent School District of Boise
1207 Fort Street
Boise, Idaho 83702

Illinois

Mr. William Rutter, Superintendent
Valley View High School District 211
Taylor Road & Route 53
Lockport, Illinois 60441

Dr. Earl J. Schurr, Superintendent
Posen-Robbins School District
No. 143½
14545 California Avenue
Posen, Illinois 60469

Mr. Raymond R. Torry, Superintendent
Washington Community High School
District 308
115 Bondurant Street
Washington, Illinois 61571

Dr. George B. Smittle, Superintendent
Community Unit School District No. 60
1020 Glen Rock Avenue
Waukegan, Illinois 60085

Indiana

Mr. Paul A. McPherson,
    Superintendent
Mississinewa Community Schools
Administration Building
424 West Main Street
Gas City, Indiana 46933

Mr. Edward H. Cuddy, Ass't. Super-
    intendent for Secondary Education
Metropolitan School District of Warren
Township
Indianapolis, Indiana 46200

Mr. Gordon V. Ruff, Superintendent
Lebanon Community School
Corporation
404 N. Meridian Street
Lebanon, Indiana 46052

Mr. Richard R. Rea, Superintendent
Western School Corporation
Russiaville, Indiana 46979

Mr. Bruce K. Moore, Superintendent
West Lafayette Community School
Corporation
1130 North Salisbury Street
West Lafayette, Indiana 47906

Iowa

Mr. Buford Garner, Superintendent
Grinnell-Newburg Community Schools
929½ Broad, Box 269
Grinnell, Iowa 50112

Dr. Roderick Bickert, Superintendent
Mason City Community Schools
120 East State
Mason City, Iowa 50401

Mr. Lyle W. Kehm, Superintendent
Urbandale Community Schools
7101 Airline Avenue
Urbandale, Iowa 50322

Kansas

Dr. Carl S. Knox, Superintendent
Lawrence Unified District No. 497
2017 Louisiana
Lawrence, Kansas 66044

Dr. Merle R. Bolton, Superintendent
Topeka Unified District No. 501
415 West Eighth
Topeka, Kansas 66603

Dr. Alvin E. Morris, Superintendent
Wichita Unified District No. 259
428 South Broadway
Wichita, Kansas 67202

Louisiana

Mr. Russell Costanza, Chairman
Nicholls High School
3820 St. Claude Avenue
New Orleans, Louisiana 70117

Maine

Mr. Gerald K. Burns, Superintendent
Old Primary School
Route #26
Gray, Maine 04039

Mr. Joseph M. McBrine, Superintendent
SAD #1
Box 429
Presque Isle, Maine 04769

Mr. H. W. Hickey, Superintendent
Westbrook Public Schools
Bridge Street
Westbrook, Maine 04092

Maryland

Dr. Roland N. Patterson,
   Superintendent
Baltimore City School District
3 East 25th Street
Baltimore, Maryland 21218

Dr. John L. Carnochan, Jr.,
   Superintendent
Frederick County School District
115 East Church Street
Frederick, Maryland 21701

Dr. Homer Elseroad, Superintendent
Montgomery County School District
850 North Washington Street
Rockville, Maryland 20850

Dr. George E. Thomas, Superintendent
Carroll County School District
County Office Building
Westmenster, Maryland 21157

Massachusetts

Mr. John Kraskouskas, Director
Bellingham Public Schools
Bellingham, Massachusetts 02019

Michigan

Mr. R. Bruce McPherson,
   Superintendent
Ann Arbor Public Schools
2555 S. State Street
Ann Arbor, Michigan 48100

Mr. Robert O. Young, Superintendent
Freeland Community Schools
710 Powley Drive
Freeland, Michigan 48623

Mr. Robert W. Coulter, Superintendent
Port Huron Area Schools
509 Stanton Street
Port Huron, Michigan 48060

Missouri

Dr. C. O. McDonald, Superintendent
Hazelwood School District
15955 New Halls Ferry Road
Florissant, Missouri 63031

Mr. Charles E. House, Superintendent
Cape Girardeau School District
61 North Clark Avenue
Cape Girardeau, Missouri 63701

Montana

Mr. Thomas Henneberg, Superintendent
Columbia Falls High School
Columbia Falls, Montana 59912

Mr. Maynard A. Olson, Superintendent
Helena High School
1300 Billings Avenue
Helena, Montana 59601

Nevada

Mr. John Blaike, Superintendent
Carson City School District
Carson City, Nevada 89701

Mr. Clifford Lawrence, Deputy
  Superintendent
Clark County School District
Las Vegas, Nevada 89100

New Hampshire

Mr. Bernard Ellis, Superintendent
Derry School District
23 South Main Street
Derry, New Hampshire 03038

New Jersey

Mr. Donald A. Watts, Superintendent
Northern Valley Regional High School
District
Administrative Offices, Closter Plaza
Closter, New Jersey 07624

Mr. John B. Geissinger, Superintendent
Tenafly School District
27 West Clinton Avenue
Tenafly, New Jersey 07670

Mr. William Meskill, Superintendent
Long Branch School District
6 West End Court, P. O. Box 1
Long Branch, New Jersey 07740

Mr. Thomas E. Harrington,
  Superintendent
Mount Laurel Township School District
Hattie Britt School
Mt. Laurel Road
Moorestown, New Jersey 08057

Mr. J. Garfield Jackson, Superintendent
East Orange School District
21 Winans Street
East Orange, New Jersey 07017

Mr. Patrick A. Torre, Superintendent
Madison Township School District
Route 516
Matawan, New Jersey 07747

Mr. Anthony J. Greco, Superintendent
Belleville School District
183 Union Avenue
Belleville, New Jersey 07109

Mr. William V. Godshall,
  Superintendent
Hanover Park Reg. HS District
161 Whippany Road
Whippany, New Jersey 07981

Mr. August W. Muller, Superintendent
Black Horse Pike Regional HS District
Erial Road
Blackwood, New Jersey 08012

Mr. Joseph A. Chinnici, Superintendent
Delran Township School District
Chester Avenue School
Delran, New Jersey 08075

Mr. Williard J. Congreve,
  Superintendent
Washington Township School District
Bunker Hill School
RFD #3
Sewell, New Jersey 80880

Mr. Eric G. Errickson, Superintendent
Warren Hills Regional District
P. O. Box 169
Washington, New Jersey 07882

Mr. James W. Lilley, Jr., Superintendent
Gloucester Township School District
Charles W. Lewis School
Davistown-Erial Roads
Blackwood, New Jersey 08012

Mr. Clyde A. Stauffer, Superintendent
Monroe Township School District
RD #2, Box 45
Cranbury, New Jersey 08512

Ohio

Mr. John Ellis, Superintendent
Columbus City Schools
270 East State Street
Columbus, Ohio 43200

Mr. Donald R. Waldrip, Superintendent
Cincinnati City Schools
230 E. 9th Street
Cincinnati, Ohio 45200

Mr. Russel Lee, Superintendent
Butler County Schools
Third & Ludlow Streets
Hamilton, Ohio 45000

Mr. Walter Smith, Superintendent
Chardon Local Schools
206 E. Park Street
Chardon, Ohio 44024

Mr. A. J. Barr, Superintendent
Madison Local Schools
6741 North Ridge Road
Madison, Ohio 44057

Oregon

Mr. Robert W. Blanchard,
  Superintendent
Portland School District No. 1
631 N. E. Clackamas Street
Portland, Oregon 97208

Mr. Delbert Fennell, Superintendent
Tigard School District No. 23J
13137 S. W. Pacific Highway
Tigard, Oregon 97223

Mr. Boyd Applegarth, Superintendent
Beaverton School District No. 48J
P. O. Box 200
Beaverton, Oregon 97005

Mr. Duane Stanbro, Superintendent
Colton School District No. 53
P. O. Box 38
Colton, Oregon 97017

Mr. Joseph Wenzel, Superintendent
Reedville School District No. 29
2425 S. W. 219th
Aloha, Oregon 97005

Mr. C. Edwin Ditto, Superintendent
Oregon City No. 62
P. O. Box 591
Oregon City, Oregon 97045

Mr. William M. Kendrick,
  Superintendent
Salem No. 24J
1309 Ferry Street, SE
Salem, Oregon 97308

Mr. Chester L. Tunnell, Superintendent
West Linn No. 3J
Administration Building
West Linn, Oregon 97068

Pennsylvania

Mr. H. Ronald Huber, Superintendent
Central Bucks School District
315 W. State Street
Doylestown, Pennsylvania 18901

Mr. John S. Sandel, Superintendent
Millcreek Township School District
3740 W. 26th Street
Erie, Pennsylvania 16506

Mr. Joseph E. Ferderbar,
  Superintendent
Neshaminy School District
Administration Building
340 E. Maple Avenue
Langhorne, Pennsylvania 19047

Mr. William E. Babcock, Superintendent
State College Area School District
131 W. Nittany Avenue
State College, Pennsylvania 16801

Mr. William H. Stoutenburgh,
  Superintendent
Wissahickon School District
Houston Road
Ambler, Pennsylvania 19002

Mr. H. Charles Shultz, Superintendent
Fairview School District
Fairview, Pennsylvania 16415

Mr. Joseph E. Shafley, Superintendent
Gateway School District
Administration Offices
Moss Side Blvd.
Monroeville, Pennsylvania 15146

Mr. Raymond L. Dunlap,
Superintendent
Manheim Township School District
School Road, Box 5134
Lancaster, Pennsylvania 17601

Rhode Island

Mr. Edward P. Travers, Superintendent
574 Hope Street
Bristol, Rhode Island 02809

Mr. John W. O'Brien, Superintendent
Narragansett School District
29 Fifth Avenue
Narragansett, Rhode Island 02887

Mr. John W. Rose, Superintendent
North Kingston School District
656 Ten Rod Road
North Kingston, Rhode Island 02852

South Carolina

Dr. Claud E. Kitchens, Superintendent
Columbia City Schools
1616 Richland Street
Columbia, South Carolina 29201

Mr. Henry L. Sneed, Superintendent
Florence City Schools
109 West Pine Street
Florence, South Carolina 29501

Mr. H. E. Corley, Superintendent
Richland District Two Schools
6831 Brookfield Road
Columbia, South Carolina 29206

South Dakota

Dr. Charles A. Lindley, Superintendent
Rapid City Public Schools
809 South Street
Rapid City, South Dakota 57701

Mr. Eldon Gran, Superintendent
Douglas School System
Ellsworth A. F. B., South Dakota 57706

Dr. J. W. Harris, Superintendent
Sioux Falls Public Schools
201 West 38th Street
Sioux Falls, South Dakota 57102

Tennessee

Mr. Walter W. Shanks, Superintendent
Putnam County Schools
442 East Spring Street
Cookeville, Tennessee 38501

Mr. Sam P. McConnell, Superintendent
Hamilton County Schools
317 Oak Street
Chattanooga, Tennessee 37403

Mr. John P. Freeman, Superintendent
Memphis City Schools
2597 Avery Avenue
Memphis, Tennessee 38112

Mr. Max H. Vann, Superintendent
Montgomery-Clarksville Schools
1209 Madison Street
Clarksville, Tennessee 37040

Ms. Mildred Doyle, Superintendent
Knox County Schools
400 W. Hill Avenue
Knoxville, Tennessee 37902

Utah

Dr. T. H. Bell, Superintendent
Granite School District
340 E. 3545 South
Salt Lake City, Utah 84115

Mr. Clarke N. Johnson, Superintendent
Tooele School District
Tooele, Utah 84074

Washington

Dr. Forbes Bottomly, Superintendent
Seattle School District No. 1
815 Fourth Avenue North
Seattle, Washington 98109

Dr. Walter Hitchcock, Superintendent
Spokane School District 81
W. 825 Trent Avenue
Spokane, Washington 99201

Mr. Ray Patrick, Superintendent
Evergreen School District 114
Route 7, 7000 NE 117th Avenue
Vancouver, Washington 98662

Dr. Robert Bates, Superintendent
Vancouver School District 37
605 No. Devine Road
Vancouver, Washington 98661

Dr. Milton Smith, Superintendent
Longview School District 122
28th and Lilac Streets
Longview, Washington 98632

Wisconsin

Mr. C. Richard Nelson, Superintendent
Racine Unified District #1
2230 Northwestern Avenue
Racine, Wisconsin 53400

Mr. Norman Fries, Superintendent
Hamilton-Sussex Public Schools
W220 N6151 Town Line Road
Sussex, Wisconsin 53089

Mr. P. R. Reinfeldt, Superintendent
Burlington Public Schools
Burlington, Wisconsin 53105

Wyoming

Mr. Leo Breeden, Assistant
    Superintendent
Cheyenne Public Schools
Cheyenne, Wyoming 82001

Dr. Joe E. Lutjeharms, Superintendent
School District No. 1
253 Prairie Avenue
Cheyenne, Wyoming 82001

*Feasibility studies were required of all district officials in California contemplating implementation of an extended school year prior to July 1, 1973.

A GENERAL BIBLIOGRAPHY

A. Books

Bouden, Haygood S. *Two Hundred Years of Education.* Richmond, Virginia: Dietz Printing Company, 1932.

Cubberley, Ellwood P. *Public Education in the United States.* Chicago: Houghton Mifflin Company, 1947.

Elsbree, Willard S. *The American Teacher.* New York: American Book Company, 1939.

Good, Carter V., ed. *Dictionary of Education.* New York: McGraw-Hill Book Company, Inc., 1959.

Hermansen, Kenneth L., and Gove, James. *The Year-Round School.* Hamden, Connecticut: Linnet Books, 1971.

Moehlman, A. B. *School Administration.* New York: Houghton Mifflin Company, 1940.

Schoenfield, Clarence A., and Schmitz, Neil. *Year-Round Education.* Madison, Wisconsin: Dembar Educational Research Services, Inc., 1964.

B. Periodicals

Adams, Andrew. "Look Hard at This Year-Round School Plan." *American School Board Journal,* 156 (July, 1968), 11-14, 31.

"Air-Conditioning Costs Decreasing." *Nation's Schools,* 63 (May, 1959), 127-128.

Allen, James E., Jr. "All-Year School—Time for a New Look?" *School Management,* 10 (February, 1966), 86-92, 146-156.

"All-Year Cure-All?" *Time,* 71 (March 10, 1958), 67.

"All-Year School." *Elementary School Journal,* 26 (September, 1925), 2-4.

"All-Year Schools." *School Executive Magazine,* 49 (July, 1930), 516-517.

"All-Year School Can Wait, Two of Three Schoolmen Assert." *Nation's Schools,* 73 (March, 1964), 84-85.

"All-Year High School—Experiment Ends in Failure." *School Management,* 10 (November, 1966), 73.

"All-Year Schools for Chicago?" *School and Society*, 22 (August 8, 1925), 165.

Ames, Robert G. "Why One District Reject Year-Round Schools." *Nation's Schools*, 84 (December, 1969), 94.

"Are Year-Round Schools Coming?" *U.S. News and World Report*, 39 (November 11, 1955), 100-103.

Association for Supervision and Curriculum Development. "Summer Programs for Students and Teachers; excerpts from Extending the School Year." *Education Digest*, 27 (1961), 26-28.

Bailey, Thomas D., and Maynard, Zollie. "Florida Youngsters Like Summer School." *School Executive*, 77 (May, 1958), 85.

Bauman, W. Scott. "Four-Quarter Plan Uses Schools All Year Long." *Nation's Schools*, 80 (November, 1967), 69-70.

Beckwith, Robert M. "Valley View 45-15 Continuous School Year Plan." *American School and University*, 43 (November, 1970), 19-28.

Bendickson, Perry. "Extend the School Year." *Instructor*, 75 (November, 1965), 98, 134.

Berman, Harvey. "Do Our Schools Need More Time?" *American School Board Journal*, 135 (November, 1957), 35-36.

Best, John W. "Year-Round School Program." *School Executive*, 73 (October, 1953), 56-59.

Beveridge, J. H. "Omaha High Schools on All-Year Plan." *School Life*, 11 (October, 1925), 22.

Bienestok, Theodore. "Resistance to an Educational Innovation." *Elementary School Journal*, 65 (May, 1965), 420-428.

Boutwell, W. D. "Summer Use of School Facilities in Riverside, California." *School Executive* (July, 1955), 62-71.

——————. "What's Happening in Education—Courses in Summer?" *National Parent Teacher*, 53 (May, 1958), 205.

Brinkerhoff, George L. "The Effects of All-Year Schooling Upon Scholarship." *Educational Method*, 10 (January, 1931), 203-209.

Brodinsky, Ben, ed. "The Twelve Month School: Six Possible Arrangements." *Education Summary* (October 1, 1967), 3.

Bruce, William C. "Year-Round Schools." *American School Board Journal*, 141 (October, 1960), 40.

Brueckner, L. J., and Distad, H. W. "The Effects of the Summer Vacation on Reading Ability of First Grade Pupils." *Journal of Educational Research*, 18 (1928), 308-314.

Bullock, Robert P. "Some Cultural Implications of Year-Round Schools." *Theory Into Practice*, 1 (June, 1962), 154-161.

"California Tries Year-Round High School." *American School and University*, 38 (February, 1966), 80.

Cardozier, V. Ray. "'For a 210-Day School Year." *Phi Delta Kappan*, 38 (March, 1957), 240-242.

Chapman, A. L. "Keep the Schools Open All Year." *School Executive*, 61 (May, 1942), 16.

Childress, Jack R., and Philippi, Harlan A. "Administrative Problems Related to the 11 or 12 Month School Year." *High School Journal*, 47 (March, 1964), 230-237.

Christian, Floyd T. "The Expanded, Extended School Year in Florida." *Compact*, 4 (December, 1970), 46-48.

Clark, Dean O. "Why Not an 11-Month School Year?" *School Executive*, 77 (March, 1958), 61.

Clarke, W. F. "All-Year Elementary School." *Elementary School Journal*, 22 (December, 1921), 286-289.

Committee on Organization and Administration, Teachers' Council, New York City. "Report on the All-Year School." *Elementary School Journal*, 30 (March, 1930), 509-518.

Compact, Editorial, 4 (December, 1970), 6.

"Compulsory Four-Quarter School Year." *Educational Leadership*, 27 (February, 1970), 533.

Cory, Robert T. "Parents Evaluate an Eleven Month Program." *Education*, 87 (November, 1966), 166-170.

Crawford, Robert M. "Advantages and Disadvantages of the Twelve-Month School" *Bulletin of the National Association of Secondary School Principals*, 42 (April, 1958), 232-234.

Croft Educational Services. "Administration: New York City Plan Three-Term High School." *Education Summary* (April 1, 1966), 2.

De Galen, F. S. "Some Thoughts on Summer Schools." *Clearing House*, 6 (May, 1932), 524-528.

Delaney, Arthur A. "Information Explosion and the Curriculum." *Education*, 86 (April, 1966), 494-497.

Dennard, Rebecca. "Twelve-Month: Four-Quarter School Year." *Journal of Health, Physical Education, Recreation*, 40 (October, 1969), 40, 57-58.

Dickens, Robert L., and Ballantyne, Robert H. "Year-Round Operation." *Educational Record*, 47 (Fall, 1966), 467-473.

Eberle, August W. "Responsive and Responsible Academic Calendar." *Journal of the National Association of Women Deans and Counselors*, 30 (Spring, 1967), 138-142.

"Eight High Schools in Atlanta, Georgia Area Will Begin Year-Round Operation Next September." *Education U.S.A.* (November 20, 1967), 68.

Elder, H. E. "The Effects of the Summer Vacation on Silent Reading Ability in the Intermediate Grades." *Elementary School Journal*,

27 (1927), 541-545.

Engh, Jeri. "Why Not Year-Round Schools?" *Saturday Review*, 49 (September 17, 1966), 82-84.

Ernst, Leonard. "The Year-Round School Faddish or Feasible?" *Nation's Schools*, 88 (November, 1971), 51-56.

Ferrand, Wilson, and O'Shea, M. V., *et al.* "The All-Year Schools of Newark, New Jersey." *Schools and Society*, 23 (April 10, 1926), 463-469.

Faunce, Roland G. "Twelve Months of School." *National Association of Secondary School Principals Bulletin*, 36 (January, 1952), 25-29.

Fawcett, N. G. "New Challenge to Education." *Theory Into Practice*, 1 (June, 1962), 125-130.

Fitzpatrick, Dave. "Why Nova School Switched to Three 70 Day Trimesters." *Nation's Schools*, 77 (April, 1966), 30, 34.

"Four Plans for Extending the School Year." *Journal of the National Education Association*, 50 (May, 1961), 55-56.

"Four-Quarter School Year." *American School Board Journal*, 141 (October, 1960), 10.

Friggens, Paul. "Year-Round Schools." *National Parent-Teacher*, 53 (April, 1959), 7-9.

Frost, Joe L. "Time to Teach." *Texas Outlook*, 51 (October, 1967), 34-35, 62.

Gallup, George M. "Fourth Annual Gallup Poll of Public Attitudes Toward Education." *Phi Delta Kappan*, 54 (September, 1972), 33-46.

Gaumitz, Walter H. "Underbuilt or Underused? A Searching Analysis of Present Day School Housing." *Clearing House*, 30 (January, 1956), 275-278.

Gillis, Reid. "The 12-Month School Year: Plans and Strategy." *Education Summary*, Croft Educational Services (September, 1968), 5-6.

Glass, Robert E. "Calendar Possibilities for Year-Round Schools." *Theory Into Practice*, 1 (June, 1962), 136-140.

Glines, Don E. "12 Month School: Is This the School of the Future?" *Instructor*, 80 (August, 1970), 72-73.

Goodlad, John I. "Societal Pressures and the Curriculum." *Educational Forum*, 23 (November, 1958), 73-80.

Greer, Edith S. and Susan L. Blachall. "The Extended School Year." (Washington, D.C.: U.S. Office of Education, 1967), p. 28.

Grieder, Calvin. "Let's Lengthen the School Year." *Nation's Schools*, 62 (August, 1958), 28-29.

Guba, Egon G. "Diffusion of Innovations." *Educational Leadership*, 25 (January, 1968), 292-295.

Hack, Walter G. "Year-Round School: A Review Essay." *Theory Into Practice*, 1 (June, 1962), 170-174.

Hamman, Henry A. "Longer School Year?" *Illinois School Journal*, 48 (Spring, 1968), 47-50.

Hanson, Earl H. "What About Twelve-Month Schools?" *Education*, 84 (February, 1964), 382.

Harding, Mrs. Richard B. "Supporting Year-Round School." *National Parent-Teacher*, 52 (December, 1957), 40.

Havighurst, R. J. "Adolescence and the Postponement of Adulthood." *School Review*, 68 (Spring, 1960), 52-62.

Hebb, Bertha Y. "Longer School Term." *American School Board Journal*, 75 (October, 1927), 134.

Hicks, Maynard. "Stevenson Story: Year-Round Educational Plan." *American School Board Journal*, 149 (August, 1964), 57-58.

"High School Dropouts." *N.E.A. Research Bulletin*, 38 (February, 1960), 11-14.

Holmes, George W., III, and Seawell, William. "Summer School Reappraised." *The American School Board Journal*, 155 (January, 1968), 10-12.

_____. "The Extended School Year—Is it Administratively Feasible?" *High School Journal*, 47 (March, 1964), 224-229.

Holt, Howard B. "Year-Round Schools and System Shock." *Phi Delta Kappan*, 54 (January, 1973), 310-311.

Holton, Samuel M., ed. "Extended School Year." *High School Journal*, 47 (March, 1964), 224-263.

Huck, C. A. "Length of the School Period." *Nebraska Education Journal*, 12 (March, 1932), 109-110.

Humphrey, Hubert H. "Let's Take Off the Padlock." *American Education*, 4 (July-August, 1968), 3.

Irons, H. S. "Utilizing Buildings and Instructional Material Twelve Months Annually." *American School Board Journal*, 88 (March, 1934), 17-19.

Irwin, Constance, *et al*. "Year-Round School Program." *Journal of the National Education Association*, 45 (February, 1956), 82-84.

James, H. Thomas. "Is Year-Round School Operation Economical?" *Theory Into Practice*, College of Education, Ohio State University, 1 (June, 1962), 141-147.

Jensen, George M. "Does Year-Round Education Make Sense?" *Compact*, 4 (December, 1970), 4-6.

_____, *et al*. "Twelve-Month School Year; Panel Discussion." *Compact*, 4 (October, 1970), 28-30.

_____. "Year-Round School: Can Boards Sidestep It Much Longer?" *American School Board Journal*, 157 (July, 1969), 8-12.

Jensen, Grant W. "Curriculum—Content and Crowding." *Bulletin of* the National Association of Secondary School Principals, 42 (February, 1959), 22-25.

Johnson, Russell D. "What Are the Evidences of Need for a Year-Round Educational Program?" *Bulletin of the National Association of Secondary School Principals*, 37 (April, 1953), 325-327.

Journal of Health-Physical Education, Recreation. "Should the School Year be Lengthened? What Effect Would This Have on the Programs of Health, Physical Education, and Recreation?" *Journal of Health-Physical Education, Recreation*, 32 (January, 1961), 6, 8.

Judd, C. H. "Year-Round School Urged for More Thorough Education." *American City*, 40 (February, 1929), 140.

Katterle, Zeno B. "How Schools Can Function in Summer Months." *The School Executive*, 67 (June, 1948), 40-42.

Klein, Helen L. "When a Twelve-Month Plan is Carried Out." *Childhood Education*, 28 (February, 1952), 262-264.

Knox, Gerald M. "Can We Afford to Educate Our Children?" *Better Homes and Gardens*, (November, 1971), 56.

Lafferty, Harry M. "Let's Keep Schools Open in Summer." *Nation's Schools*, 48 (July, 1951), 41-42.

Lambert, Sam M. "Educational Growth and Change." *National Educational Association Journal*, 49 (December, 1960), 45-47.

"Length of School Year and School Day." *NEA Research Bulletin*, 43 (December, 1965), 103-105.

"Length of the School Year in Cities." *School and Society*, 30 (November, 1929), 637.

"Lengthening the School Year: Superintendent's Opinion." *Nation's Schools*, 62 (December, 1958), 6.

Letson, John W. "Atlanta Has Begun." *Compact*, 4 (December, 1970), 15-17.

Lipson, Shirley. "The Dilemma of the Year-Round School." *Theory Into Practice*, 1 (June, 1962), 121-124.

Litchfield, Edward Harold. "Trimester: Education of Superior Quality in a Shorter Length of Time." *College and University Business*, 31 (July, 1961), 24-27.

Lombardi, John. "The Los Angeles Study of Year-Round Operation." *Theory Into Practice*, 1 (June, 1962), 131-135.

"Los Angeles Rejects Plan for Keeping Schools Open Year Round: Calls it Costly, Inconvenient." *Nation's Schools*, 55 (February, 1955), 120-122.

MacPherson, Vernon D. "Keeping Schools Open All Year." *Nation's Schools*, 56 (September, 1955), 51-54.

Mallory, Stephen R. "Year-Round Schools: Coming, Coming, Here!" *School Management*, 15 (August, 1971), 24-26.

May, Frank B. "Year-Round School: A Proposal." *Elementary School Journal*, 61 (April, 1961), 388-393.

McIntosh, William R. "Year-Round Programs of Professional Services." *Educational Leadership*, 8 (February, 1951), 286-289.

_____. "Many Faces of the Twelve Month School." *Illinois Education*, 23 (May, 1961), 393-395.

McLain, John D. "Developing Flexible All-Year Schools." *Educational Leadership*, 28 (February, 1971), 472-475.

_____. "Emerging Plans for Year-Round Education." *Compact*, 4 (December, 1970), 7-8.

_____. "The Flexible All-Year School." *Research-Learning Center*, (1969).

Merwin, Willard V. "A Trimester Plan." *American School Board Journal*, 146 (April, 1963), 15.

Miles, Dorothy. "Lexington's Year-Round School." *American School Board Journal*, (March, 1952).

Miller, Richard D. "Year-Round School: Are You Ready?" *Indiana School Board Journal*, 18 (March/April, 1972).

Morgan, L. D. "How Effective is Special Training in Preventing Loss Due to Summer Vacation?" *Journal of Educational Psychology*, 20 (1929), 446-471.

Morrison, J. C. "What Effect Has the Summer Vacation on Children's Learning and Ability to Learn?" *Educational Research Bulletin*, 3 (1924), 245-249.

National Education Association. "The Advance of the American School System." *Research Bulletin*, 5 (September, 1927), 195-222.

_____. "Trends in City School Organization." *Research Bulletin*, 28 (1949), 4-39.

_____. "Length of the School Year and School Day." *Research Bulletin*, 43 (December, 1965), 103-105.

"News Front: An 11-Month School Year is Recommended in a Four-Year Study by the New York State Education Department." *Education U.S.A.* (April, 1, 1968).

"New Evidence As to the Efficiency of the All-Year School." *Elementary School Journal*, 32 (November, 1931), 168-172.

Nolte, M. Chester. "Rapid Growth of Summer Schools Poses Additional Legal Problems." *The American School Board Journal*, 152 (May, 1966), 60-61.

Ogden, Clyde L. "Four-Quarter Plan, How Practical An Idea?" *American School Board Journal*, 133 (July, 1956), 19-21, and (August, 1956), 19-21.

Ogg. T. W. "Change Affects the Rural Community." *Educational Leadership*, 17 (February, 1960), 279-281.

Oldham, Francis H. "Length of the School Day and the School

Year." *Bulletin of the National Association of Secondary School Principals*, 46 (September, 1962), 194-198.

O'Rourke, Joseph. "The Extended School Year: A Teacher View." *Theory Into Practice*, 1 (June, 1962), 166-169.

Page, F. J. "Twelve-Months Rural School" *Journal of Education*, 112 (October 27, 1930), 320.

Palm, Rueben R., and Ylorsker, H. L. "How Effective is the All-Year Secondary School." *Bulletin of the National Association of Secondary School Principals*, 34 (April, 1950), 63-67.

Pahl, Eleanor. "A Year-Round Program." *Childhood Education*, 24 (October, 1947), 82-84.

Patterson, M. V., and Rensselaer, N. Y. "The Effects of the Summer Vacation on Children's Mental Ability and on Their Retention of Arithmetic and Reading." *Education*, 46 (1925), 222-228.

Penk, G. L., and Verner, G. F. "Let's Look Before We Leap." *American School Board Journal*, 139 (October, 1959), 21-22.

Plank, Karl. "Year Round Schools: Are You Interested?" *Indiana School Board Journal*, 18 (March-April, 1972), 10.

Postel, H. H. "Enforced Idleness Abstract." *Elementary School Journal*, 29 (May, 1929), 653-654.

Pulliam, R. "All-Year Schools, Who's Right?" *Education*, 52 (November, 1931), 159-162.

Ragsdale, C. E. "9 to 3 for Nine Months." *Educational Leadership*, 1 (April, 1944), 409-412.

Redmond, James. "How to Get Your Feet Wet." *School Management*, 10 (February, 1966), 146-147.

Rich, K. W. "Present Status of the All-Year Secondary School." *California Journal of Secondary Education*, 31 (January, 1956), 18-24.

Robinson, H. M. "Year-Round Schools Again?" *Elementary School Journal*, 57 (May, 1957), 420.

Roe, W. A. "All Year Schools." *School Executive Magazine*, 50 (November, 1930), 121-123.

_____ . "All-Year Schools a Potential Progressive Educational Environment." *Educational Methods*, 10 (October, 1930), 3-6.

_____ . "All-Year School Organization." *Educational Methods*, 10 (November, 1930), 66-69.

_____ . "Comparative Costs of Integrated All-Year Schooling and of Part-Time Schooling." *Educational Methods*, 10 (March, 1931), 350-358.

_____ . "Cost Sheets and Quantity Production in Education." *Bulletin of the Department of Elementary School Principals*, 5 (April, 1926), 147.

Rogers, A. R., Jr. "A Primer on Summer Schools." *American School Board Journal*, 140 (April, 1960), 21.

Scala, Anthony W. "Year-Round School." *Bulletin of the National Association of Secondary School Principals*, 54 (March, 1970), 79-89.

"Schoolmen Visualize Need for Extended School Year; School Administrators' Opinion Poll." *Nation's Schools*, 83 (March, 1969), 101.

School Review. "The All-Year School." *School Review*, 37 (March, 1929), 174-175.

Sessions, E. B. "Maintenance and Operational Costs in a Year-Round Program." *Theory Into Practice*, 1 (June, 1962), 148-153.

"Shall We Change the School Calendar." *National Parent-Teacher*, 52 (October, 1957), 12-14.

Shane, Harold G. "In-Service Education and Personel Policies." *Nation's Schools*, 50 (September, 1952), 87-88.

Shankland, S. D. "The Need for Outdoor Education Today." *The Bulletin of the National Association of Secondary School Principals*, 30 (May, 1947), 9-12.

Shrepel M., and Laslett, H. R. "On the Loss of Knowledge by Junior High School Pupils Over the Summer Vacation." *Journal of Educational Psychology*, 27 (1936), 299-303.

Snow, W. B. "Boston School Calendar." *Elementary School Journal* (October, 1927), 134-136.

"Something About the All-Year School." *American School Board Journal*, 80 (May, 1930), 67-132.

"State Action—Extending the School Year." *Compact*, 4 (December, 1970), 4-6.

"Status of Year-Round School Programs." *School Executive*, 72 (November, 1952), 82.

Sternig, John. "Roundup on the Year-Round School." *National Education Association Journal*, 47 (January, 1958), 47-48.

——————. "Teacher Selection." *Illinois Education Association Journal*, 43 (April, 1955), 296-298.

——————. "The All-Year Program." *School Executive*, 68 (April, 1949), 66-68.

Stonecipher, J. E., and William M. Kulstad. "How Can Summer Schools Improve the Total School Program?" *National Association of Secondary School Principals Bulletin*, 42 (April, 1958), 31-36.

Studebaker, John W. "Why Not a Year-Round Educational Program?" *The Journal of Educational Sociology*, 21 (January, 1948), 269-275.

"Summer Use of School Facilities." *School Executive*, 74 (July, 1955), 62-71.

"Superintendents Reject All-Year School Plan; Opinion Poll." *Nation's Schools*, 55 (May, 1955), 6.

"Supervisor Remarks: What Is Your Opinion of a Twelve-Month School Year?" *Catholic School Journal*, 65 (May, 1965), 60.

Szuberla, Charles A. "Summer's Time for Kindergarten." *American School Board Journal*, 153 (July, 1966), 7.

_____ . "Year-Round School Evolution." *The American School Board Journal*, 155 (January, 1968), 13.

Taylor, D. E. "Year-Round School." *School Executive*, 65 (December, 1945), 50-51.

"The All-Year School." *School Review*, 37 (March, 1929), 174-175.

"The All-Year School." *School Executive*, 50 (November, 1930), 121-123.

"The All-Year School, Time for a New Look?" *School Management*, 10 (February, 1966), 86-92, 146-151, 154, 156.

"The New Trend: Year-Round Schools." *U. S. News and World Report* (July 26, 1971), 35-37.

Thomas D. R. "Implications of Demographic Changes for Education." *Phi Delta Kappan*, 41 (June, 1960), 383-385.

Thomas, George Isaiah. "The Legal and Financial Question." *Compact*, 4 (December, 1970), 9-14.

Thomas, James H. "Is Year-Round School Operation Economical?" *Theory Into Practice*, College of Education, Ohio State University, 1 (June, 1962), 141-147.

Thomas, Maurice J. "Returns on a Year-Round Investment." *Educational Leadership*, 5 (April, 1948), 459-464.

Thomas, Maurice J. "Year-Round Service and Higher Salaries." *School Executive*, 66 (April, 1947), 63-64.

Thompson, J., and L. Meyer. "What Research Says About Acceleration." *Journal of Secondary Education*, 36 (May, 1961), 302.

Tomancik, Mary. "Administrators Dispute Arguments for All-Year Schools." *Nation's Schools*, 47 (June, 1951), 69-71.

Tiffany, Burton C. "Year-Round Schools: Coming, Coming, Here!" *School Management* (August, 1971), 24-25, 27.

"Trimester Plan Makes Nova Novel." *Nation's Schools*, 73 (April, 1964), 84-88.

Tsitrian, John. "The Furgeson Plan for All-Year School." *Phi Delta Kappan*, 54 (January, 1973), 314-315.

"U. S. Near the Bottom in School Year Length." *Phi Delta Kappan,*
46 (September, 1964), 36.

Vanderslice, H. R. "Five Years' Experience With the All-Year
School." *Elementary School Journal,* 34 (December, 1933), 256-268.

——————. "The All-Year School in Aliquippa, Pennsylvania."
Elementary School Journal, 30 (April, 1930), 576-585.

——————. "What One Town Learned in Ten Years of Year-
Round Schools." *U. S. News and World Report,* 43 (August 2,
1957), 48-51.

Wagner, F. B. "Twelve-Month School." *Bulletin of the National
Association of Secondary School Principals,* 40 (April, 1956),
218-220.

Wagner, Marjorie A. "Glencoe's Summer Program Has Two Aims
—Competence and Enrichment." *Nation's Schools,* 64 (October,
1959), 58-63.

Walker, K. E. "The 3 + 3 + 3 Plan." *Clearing House,* 32 (December,
1957), 201.

Wallace, C. E. "Flexible Scheduling for the School Year." *Journal
of Secondary Education,* 37 (March, 1962), 132-135.

Weber, H. O. "The All-Year School." *Journal of Education,* 30
(October 18, 1926), 347-351.

White, Richard E. "A Board Member Looks at the Extended School
Year." *Education,* 88 (March, 1968), 245-248.

White, William D. "Year-Round Education for K-12 Districts." *Phi
Delta Kappan,* 54 (January, 1973), 312-313.

Whitcomb, Mildred. "Rural Groups Seek Quality Education."
Nation's Schools, 62 (December, 1958), 59.

Wilson, H. H. "Educational Implementations of the Nation's Manpower Needs," *School Review,* 65 (Spring, 1957), 35-40.

Wirt, W. A. "A School Year of Twelve Months." *Education,* 27 (June,
1907), 619-622.

Woods, Bob G. "Evaluating Summer School Programs." *Bulletin,
The National Association of Secondary School Principals,* 50
(March, 1966), 38-46.

Wyman, Raymond. "Full Employment of Teachers and Schools."
American School Board Journal, 135 (July, 1957), 25-26.

"Year-Round Schools—An Idea That's Coming Back." *U. S. News
and World Report,* 42 (March 1, 1957), 32-34.

"Year-Round School: Is It Successful?" *Indiana School Board
Journal,* 18 (March, April, 1972), 32-34.

"Year-Round Schools Can Reduce Cost." *Education U. S. A.*
(October, 1972), 49.

"Year-Round School: Park School, Hayward, California." *Instruc-*

tor, 79 (March, 1970), 36-38.

"Year-Round School—Report on the Latest Test." *U. S. News and World Report*, 67 (August 18, 1969), 32-34.

"Year-Round School—Report on the Latest Test." *U. S. News and World Report*, 42 (March 1, 1957), 32-34.

"Year-Round Schools Spread Across Country." *Indiana Teacher*, 116 (Summer, 1972), 109.

Ylvisaker, H. L. "How Effective Is the All-Year Secondary School?" *Bulletin, National Association of Secondary School Principals*, 34 (April, 1950), 67-73.

C. Unpublished Materials

Bureau of Administrative Leadership Services, Pennsylvania Department of Education, *Year-Round Schools*. Harrisburg: Pennsylvania Department of Education, July, 1967, revised February, 1971, 3. (Mimeographed.)

———————— . Pennsylvania Department of Education, *Year-Round Schools*, Forward by B. Anton Hess. Pennsylvania Department of Education, July, 1971, iii. (Mimeographed.)

Greer, Edith S., and Blackall, Susan L. "The Extended School Year." Washington: U. S. Office of Education, 1967. (Mimeographed.)

Gregory, Louis P. "An Evaluation of the Organization, Administration, and Financing of the Extended Public School Program for Metropolitan Areas of Florida." Unpublished Ed. D. dissertation, University of Florida, 1954.

Hirshey, Charles E. "An Analysis and Appraisal of Selected Aspects of the Summer Enrichment Programs in the Public Schools of Florida." Unpublished Ed. D. dissertation, University of Pittsburgh, 1959.

Kurtman, David H. "Breaking the Tradition." *Year-Round Schools*. Harrisburg: Bureau of Administrative Leadership Service, Pennsylvania Department of Education, July, 1967, revised February, 1971, ii. (Mimeographed.)

Lawrie, Jack Douglas. "The Feasibility of Extending the Secondary School Year in North Carolina." Unpublished Ed. D. dissertation, Duke University, 1961.

Lewis, Russel F. *The Organization and Administration of Summer Public School Educational and Recreational Programs in Districts Within Metropolitan Areas of the United States*. Unpublished Doctoral dissertation, University of Southern California, 1940.

Lydich, Frank J. Remarks to the Senate Education Committee on Year-Round Schools. Harrisburg, Pennsylvania, October 8, 1971, 3-4. (Mimeographed.)

Norris, J. A., Jr. "Position taken by Governors pertaining to School Term Extension as a Factor in the Equalization of Rural and City Educational Opportunity in the Public Schools of North Carolina, 1924-1943." Unpublished Doctoral dissertation, Duke University, 1963.

Pappalardo, Peter Anthony. "A Study of Acceptability and Practicality of Adopting a Twelve-Month School Year for Public Schools of Dade County, Florida." Unpublished Doctoral dissertation, University of Miami (Florida), 1969.

Quick, G. L. "The Advantage of Extending the School Year." Unpublished Doctoral dissertation, The University of Nebraska Teachers College, 1966.

Reifschneider, Robert H. "The Extended School Year Program." Unpublished Ed. D. dissertation, Teachers' College, University of Nebraska, 1958.

Sales, Mildred Vance. "The Status of the Public Summer High School in North Carolina." Unpublished Ed. D. dissertation, Duke University, 1960.

Scala, Anthony W. "Survey of the History and Current Status of the ESY in Selected Schools." Unpublished Doctoral dissertation, St. John's University, 1968.

Shedd, Arthur B. "To What Extent and in What Ways Are the Plants and Personnel of American Public High Schools Used for the Education of Youth During the Summer Months?" Unpublished Ed. D. dissertation, Teachers' College, Columbia University, 1950.

Shreve, Robert H. "A Survey of Selected Schools Currently Operating Extended School-Year Programs." Unpublished Ed. D. dissertation, Colorado State College, 1955.

Sutton, Wayne M. "Year-Round Evaluation in Public Schools." Unpublished Doctoral dissertation, University of Illinois, 1970.

Whittier, C. Taylor. "The Twelve-Four Plan—A Preliminary Report," Rockville, Maryland: Board of Education of Montgomery County, 1961. (Mimeographed.)

Year Round Schools. Harrisburg: Bureau of Administrative Leadership Service, Pennsylvania Department of Education, 1967, revised, 1971. (Mimeographed.)

D. Publications of the Government, Learned Societies and Other Organizations

American Association of School Administrators. *Year-Round School.* Washington: The Association, 1960.

American Association of School Administrators. *The Year-Round*

School. Washington: The Association, 1970.

Connor, Forrest E., and W. J. Ellena. *The Year-Round School.* American Association of School Administrators, 1970.

Cuddy, Edward H. *The Year-Round School or the Rescheduled School Year: A Study for the Board of Education Metropolitan School District of Warren Township.* Indianapolis: Wayne Township Independent School District, 1969.

Florida Educational Research and Development Council. *Year-Round School for Polk County, Florida: A Feasibility Study.* Gainesville: Florida Educational Research and Development Council, College of Education, University of Florida, 1966.

Florida State Department of Education. *The All-Year School.* Tallahassee: Department of Education, April, 1957.

Hurnard, John R. "Extending the Scope of the School: Considerations for Reorganizing the School Year." *Oregon School Study Council Bulletin.* College of Education, University of Oregon: Eugene, Oregon, 1972.

Ikeda, Carole M. *The Implication of Year-Round Education for Hawaii's Public Schools.* Honolulu: Legislative Reference.

Indiana State Department of Education. *Division of Planning and Evaluation. Year-Round School Profiles and Information.* Indianapolis, Indiana, February 21, 1972. (Mimeographed.)

Johns, Roe L., *et al.* "Extended School Year." *Dimensions of Educational Needs*, National Educational Finance Project, 1969, Chapter 8, pp. 191-205.

McLain, John D., and Means, Don. *Current Status of Year-Round Education in America.* Clarion, Pennsylvania: Educational Development Center for Year-Round Education, Clarion State College, 1973.

National Educational Association, Research Division. *The Rescheduled School Year.* Washington: The Association, 1968.
＿＿＿＿＿＿＿ . "Year-Round Employment for Teachers." Washington: The Association, 1951.

National School Public Relations Association. *Year-Round School: Districts Develop Successful Programs.* Washington: National School Public Relations Association, 1971.

Pennsylvania Chamber of Commerce. "Year-Round Education." *Legislative Spotlight.* Harrisburg: Pennsylvania Chamber of Commerce, April 30, 1971.

Proceedings of the Third National Seminar on Year-Round Education. Cocoa Beach, Florida, 1971.

Status of the Extended School Year in 1972. Tallahassee: College of Education, University of Florida, 1972.

"The 12-Month School." *Mississinewa Community Schools*, Gas City, Indiana, 1971.

The State University of New York/State Education Department, Office of Research and Evaluation. *Extended School Year Designs*, 1966.

The University of The State of New York/The State Education Department. *Setting the Stage for Lengthened School Year Programs.* New York: 1968.

Weber, H. O. "Defense Through the Educated Quota; The All-Year School." *National Education Association Addresses and Proceedings*, 63 (1925), 751-759.

E. Encyclopedia

Cubberley, E. "Vacation Schools and Continuous Sessions of Public Schools." *Encyclopedia of Education*, ed. Monroe, 5. New York: The MacMillan Co., 1913.

Otto, Henry J. "Elementary Education—Organization and Administration," in Walter S. Monroe, ed., *Encyclopedia of Educational Research*, New York: MacMillan Company, 1950.

INDEX